AF618075

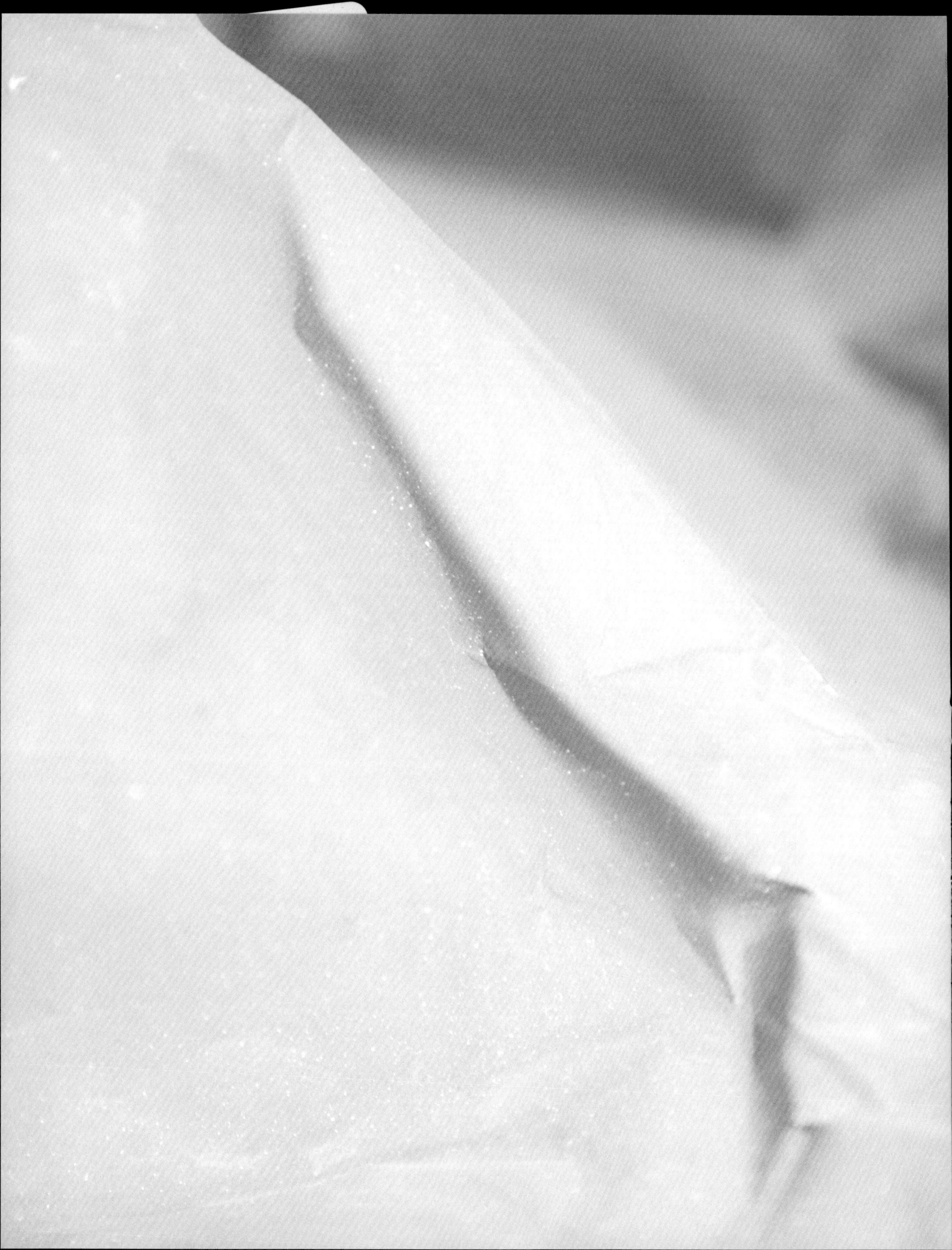

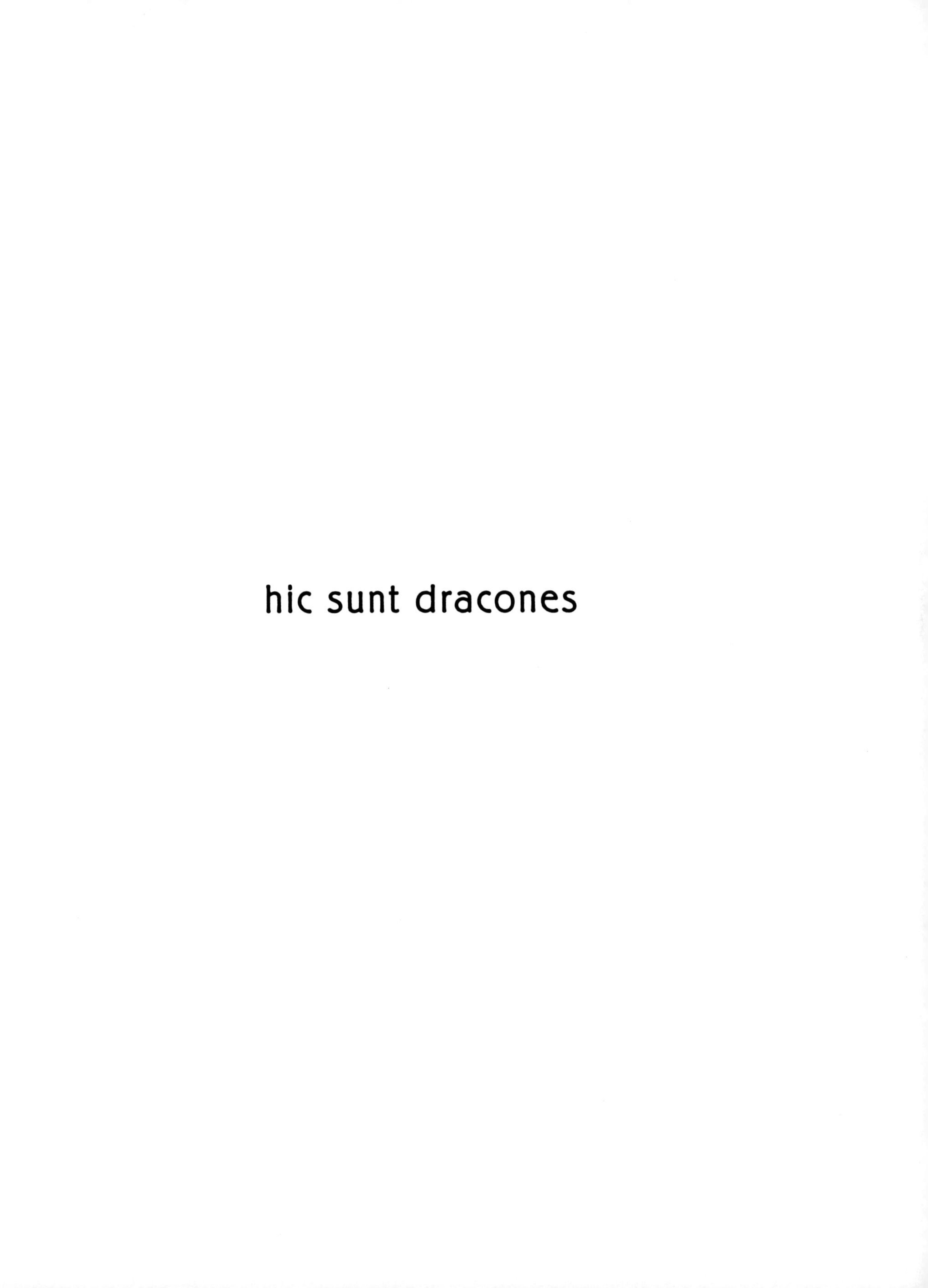

hic sunt dracones

mit freundlicher Unterstützung von /
with the kind support of

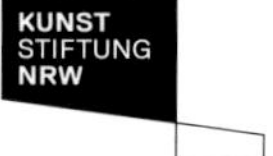

hic sunt dracones

MAREN MAURER

DISTANZ

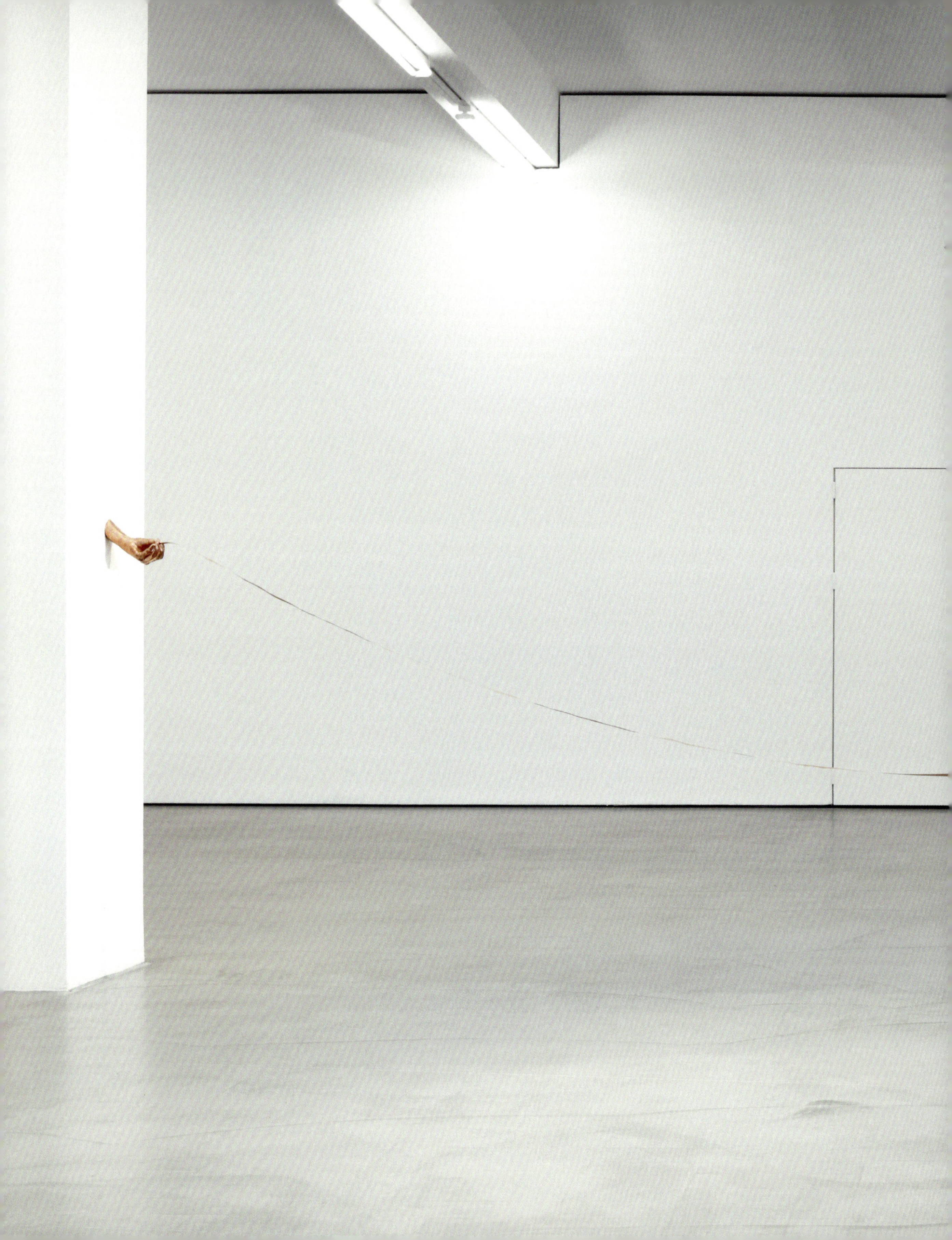

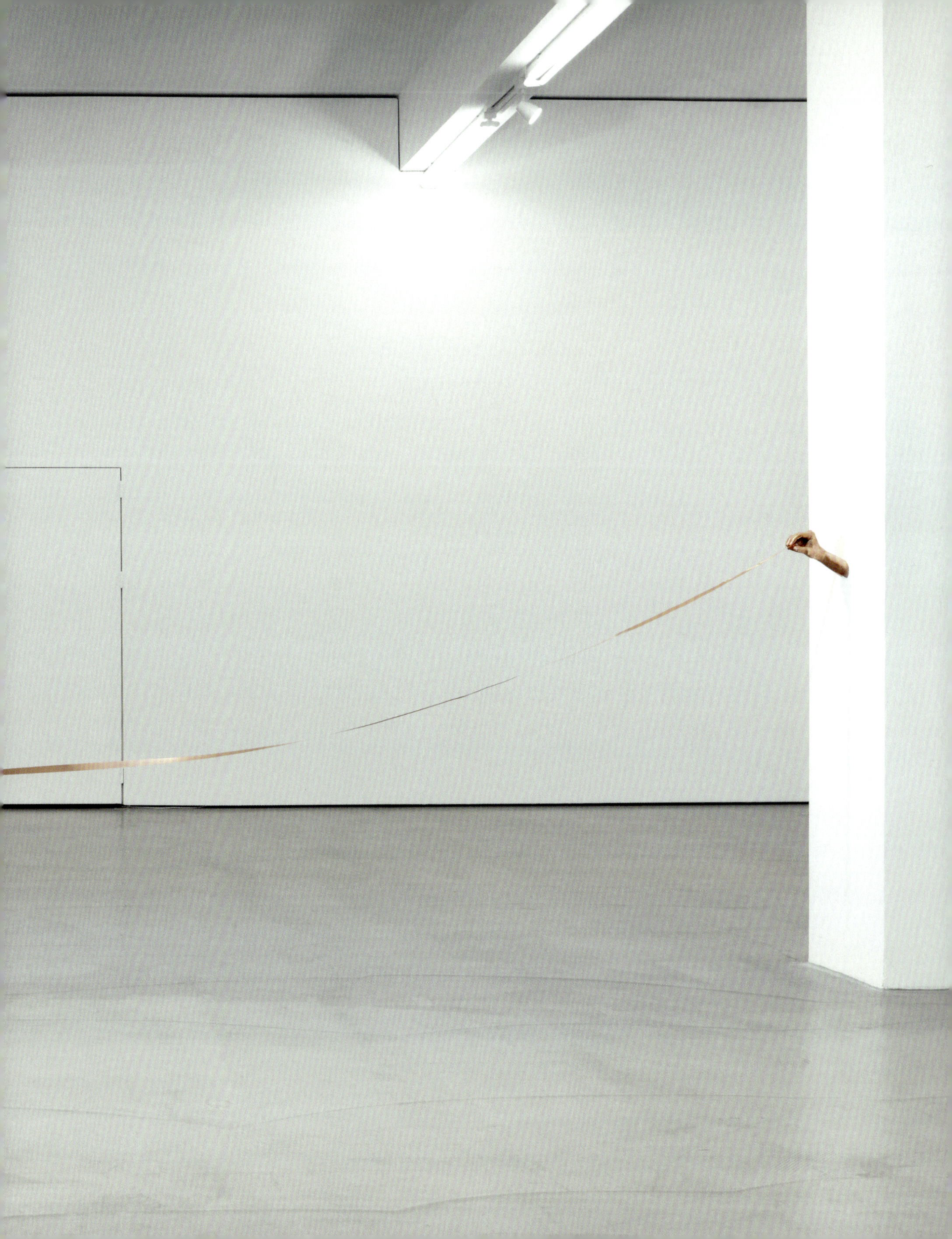

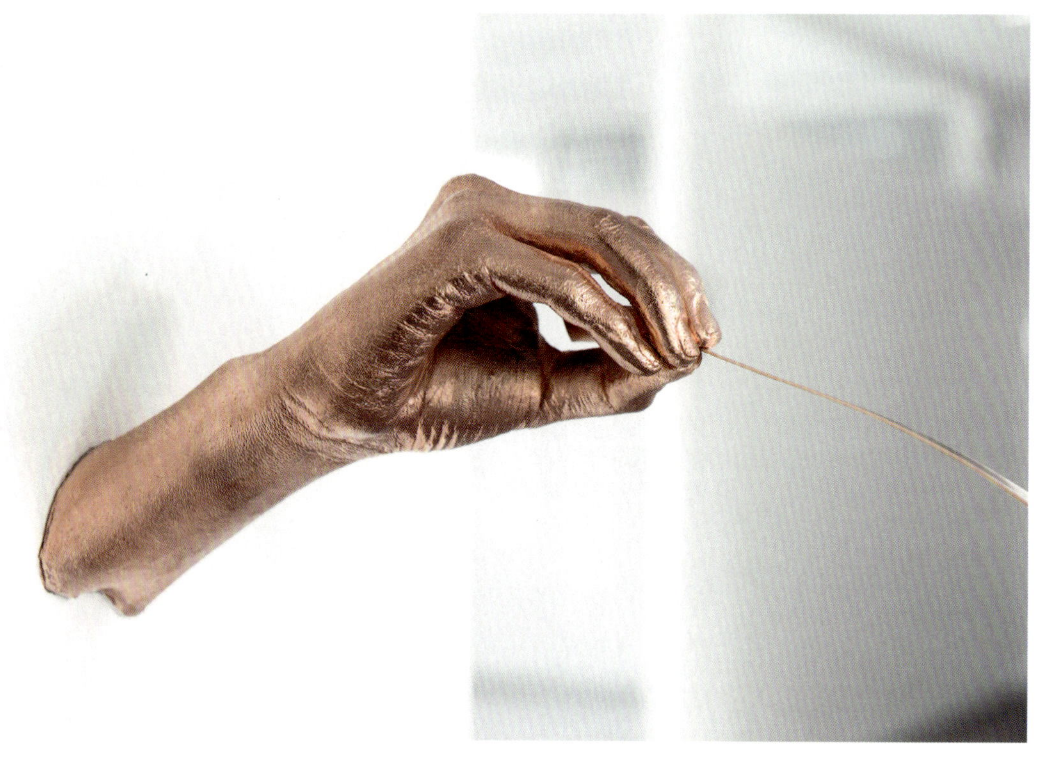

S. / pp. 4–6

ICH , WAS, 2011
coppered bronze, copper band
dimensions variable
Installation COSAR HMT (S. / pp. 4–5) and former
American Embassy (S. / p. 6)

INHALT / CONTENTS

ANNABELLE, 2013
patinized bronze on pedestal
29 x 21 x 40 cm

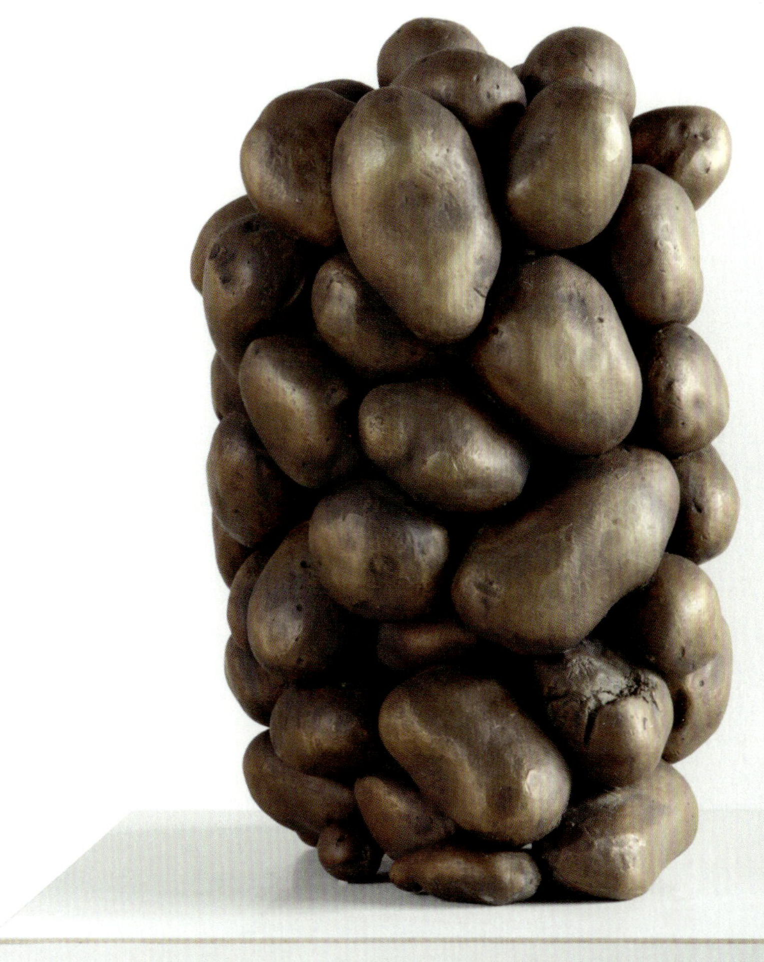

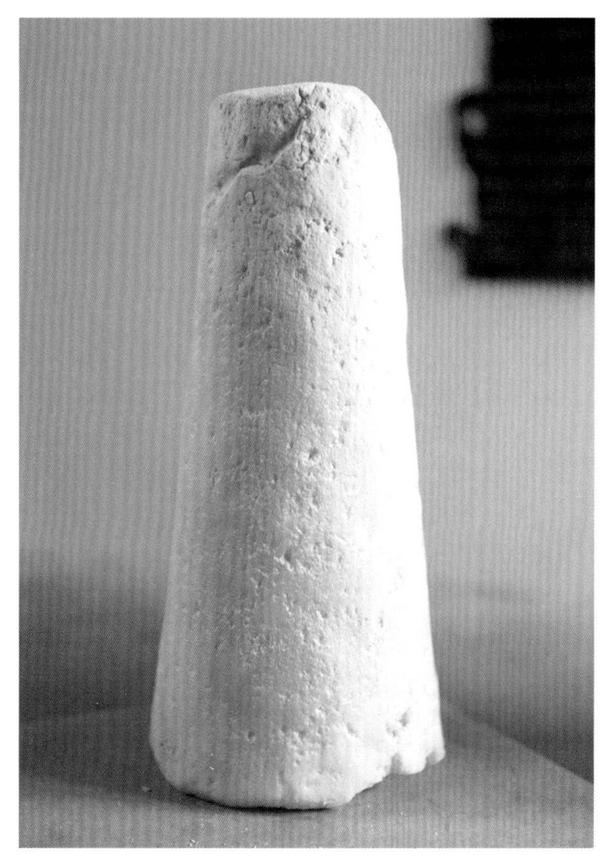

SUGAR, 2013
pigmented wax on pedestal
36,5 x 47 cm

AUGUSTE VICTORIA, 2013
patinized bronze on pedestal
28 x 21 x 40 cm

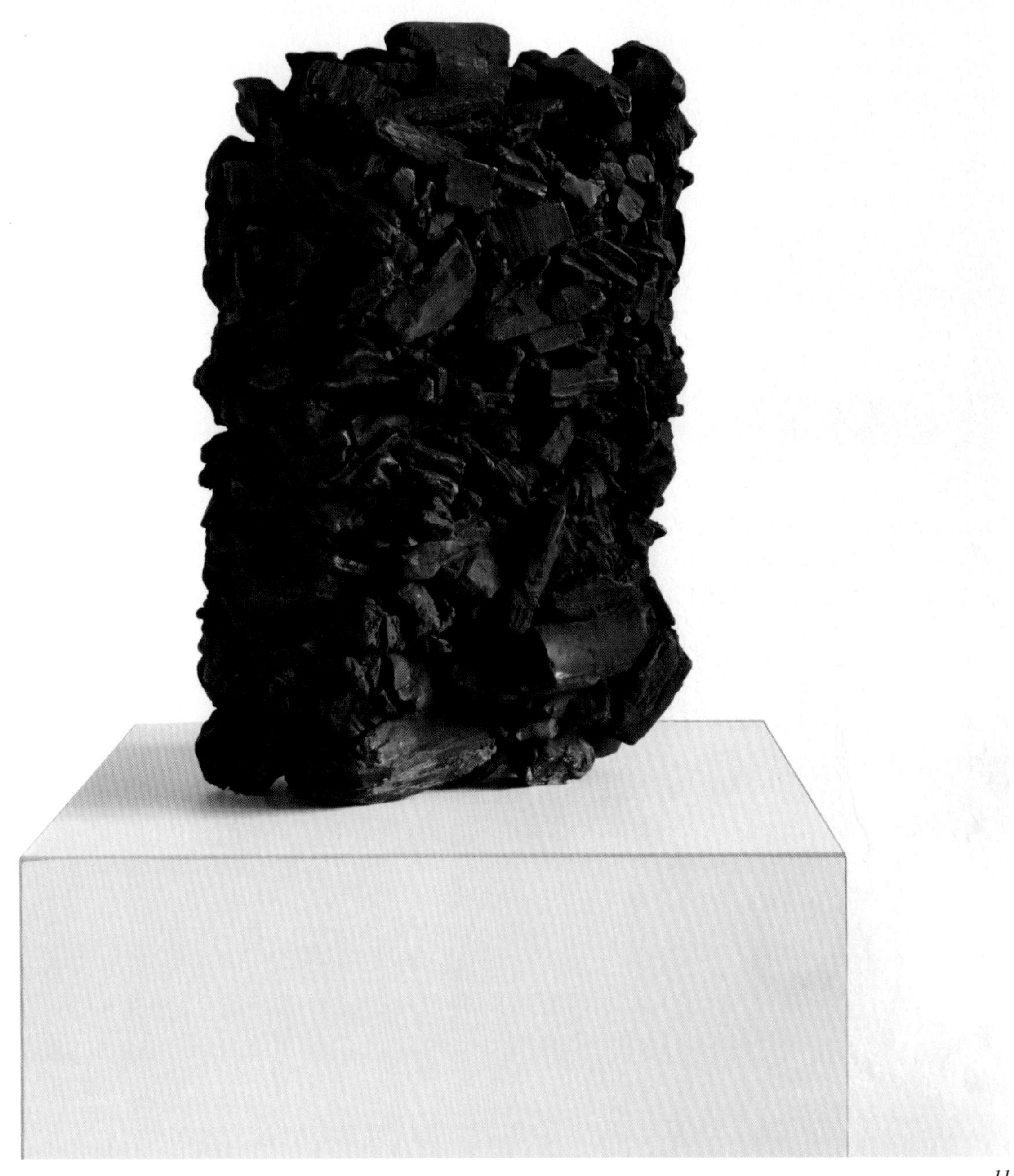

CAKE, 2013
aluminium, varnished wood
72 x 67 x 18 cm

S. / pp. 14–15

MIRROR, MIRROR, 2014
aluminium
97 x 79 cm

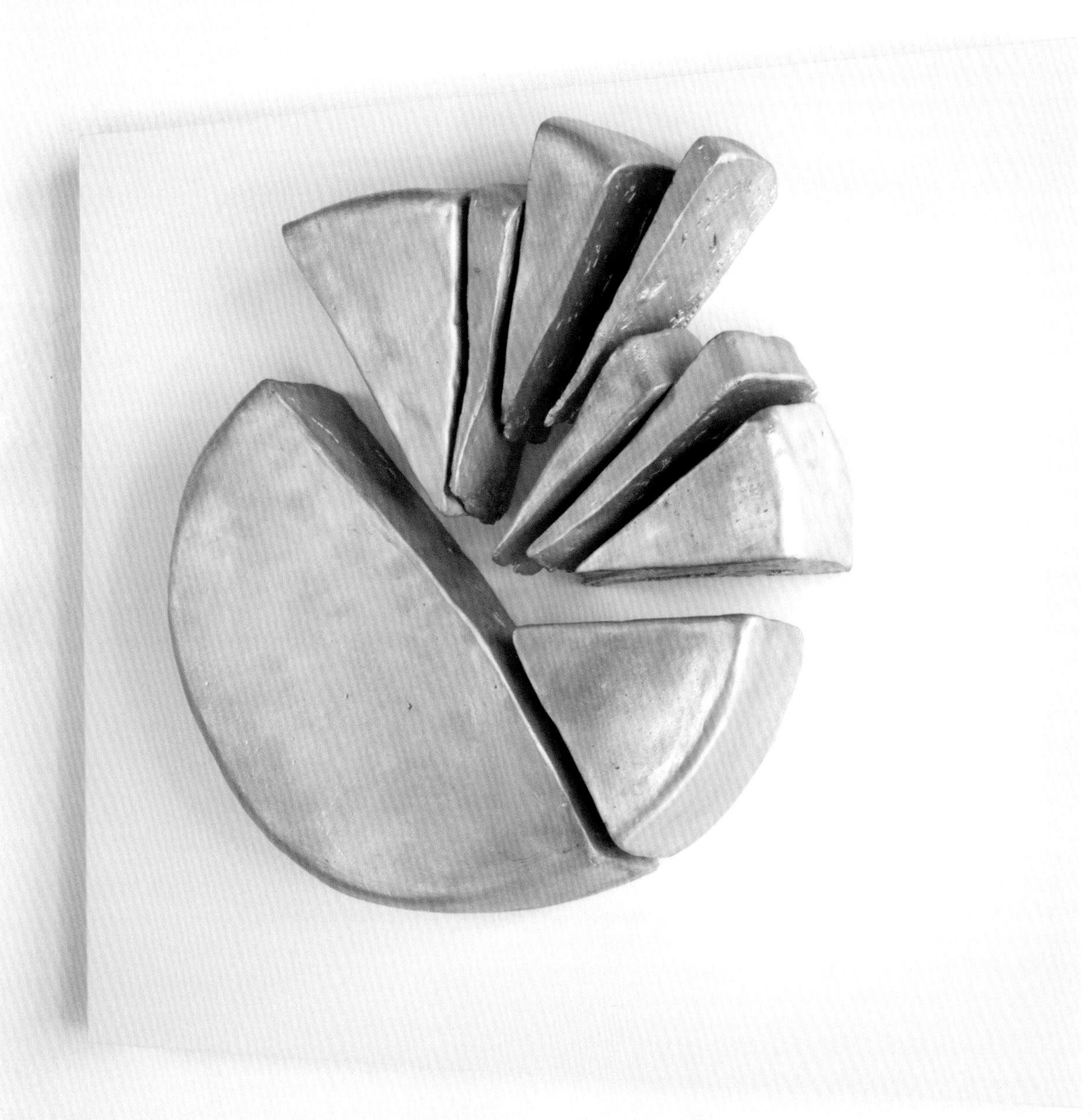

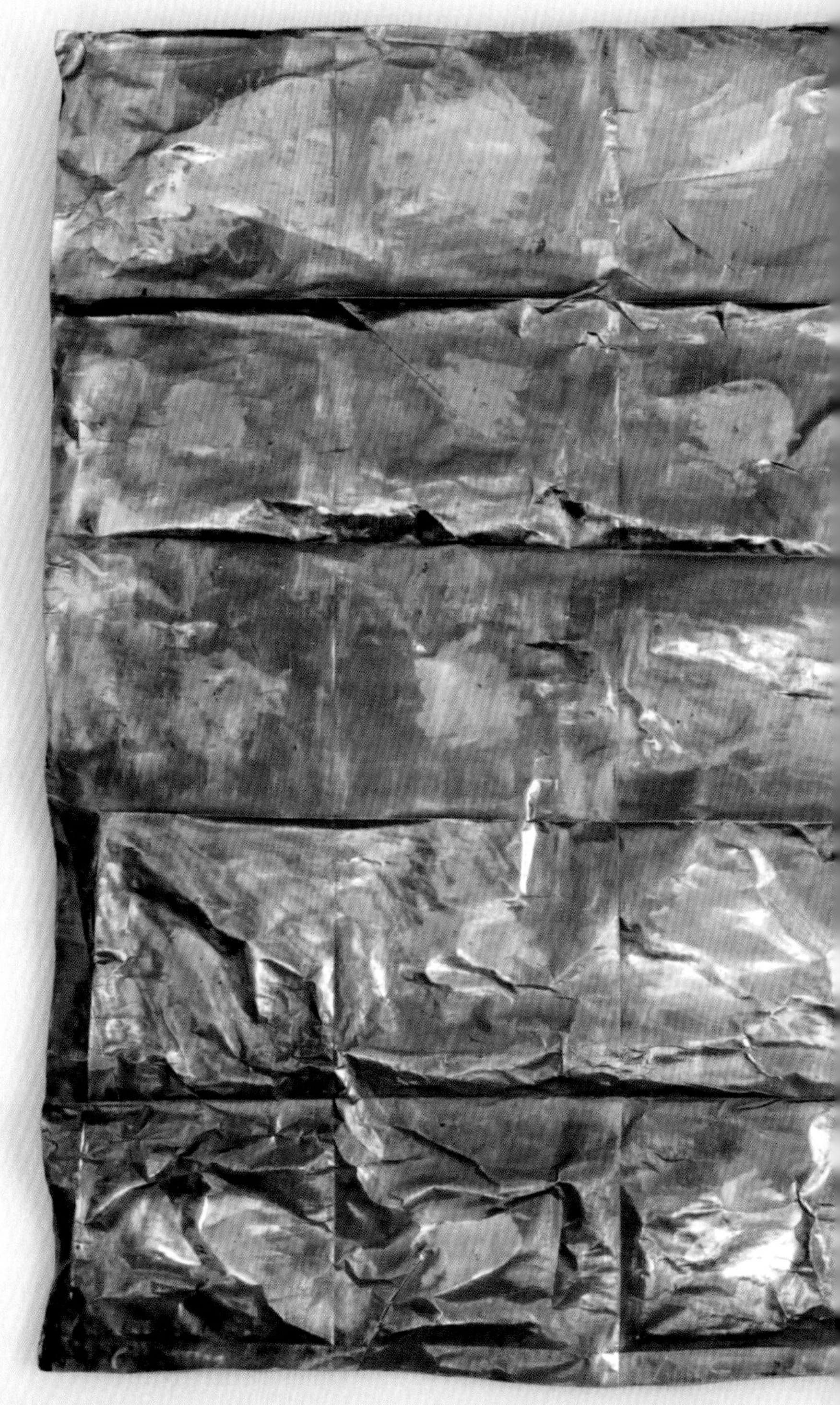

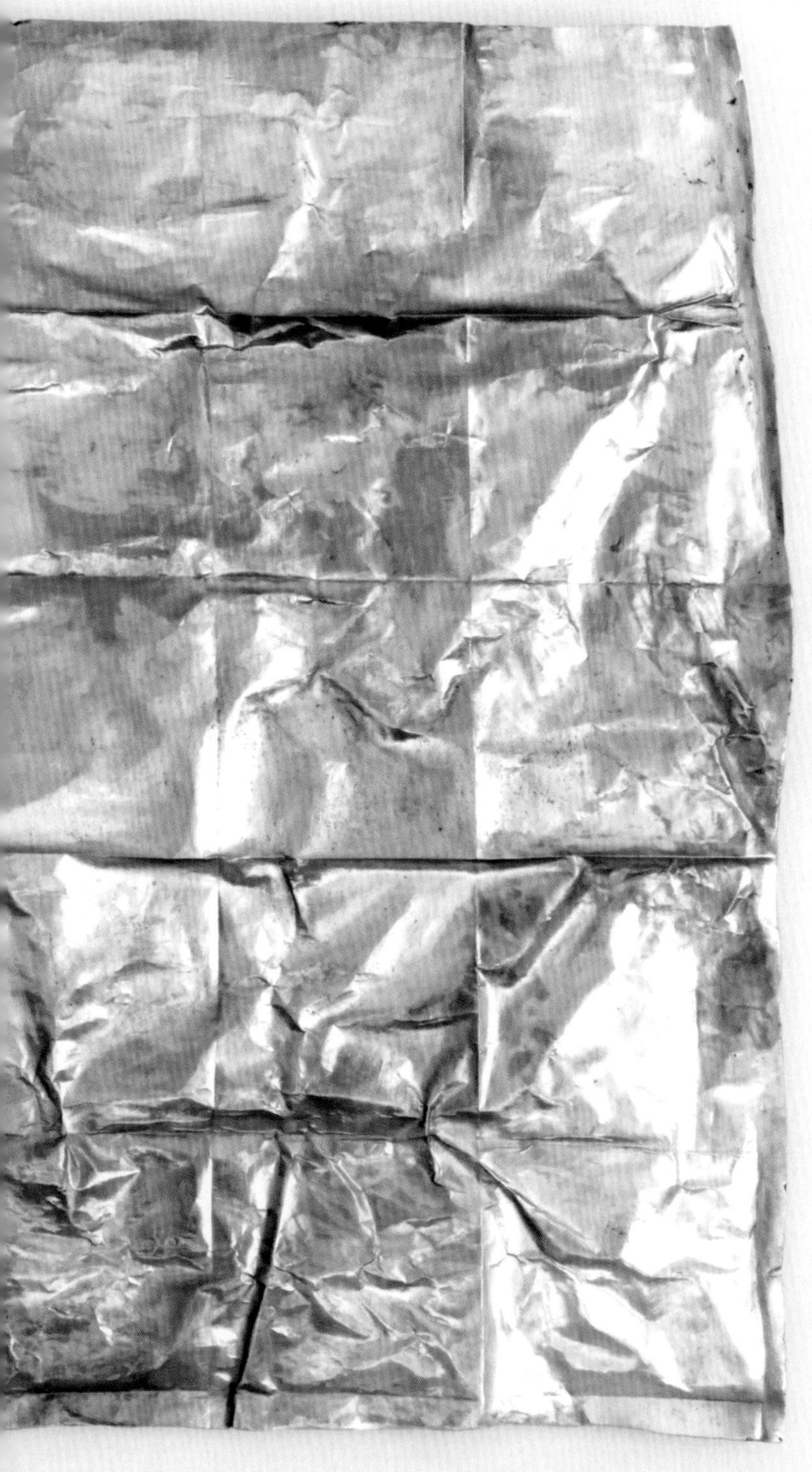

GEWISSER AUFSTAND, 2015
leather, rubber, styrofoam, mortar
height 101 cm, Ø 53 cm

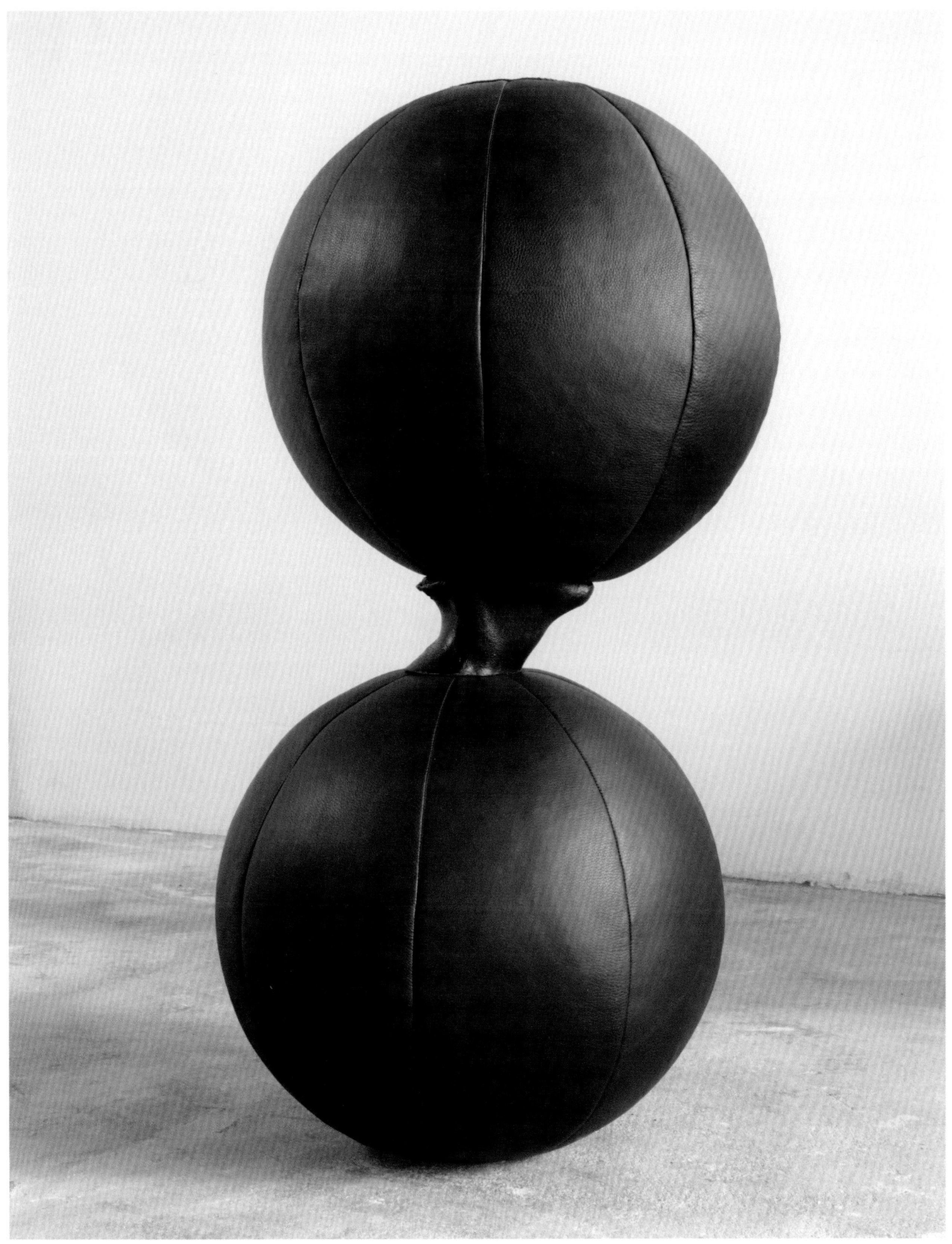

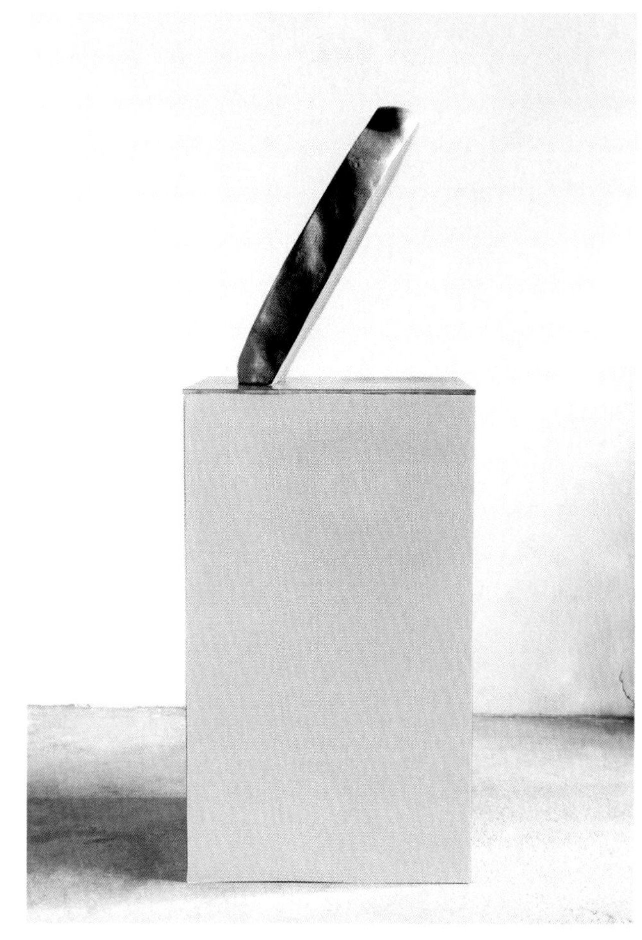

DIAGONAL (DAVID), 2014
patinized bronze, steel on pedestal
58 x 57 x 51 cm

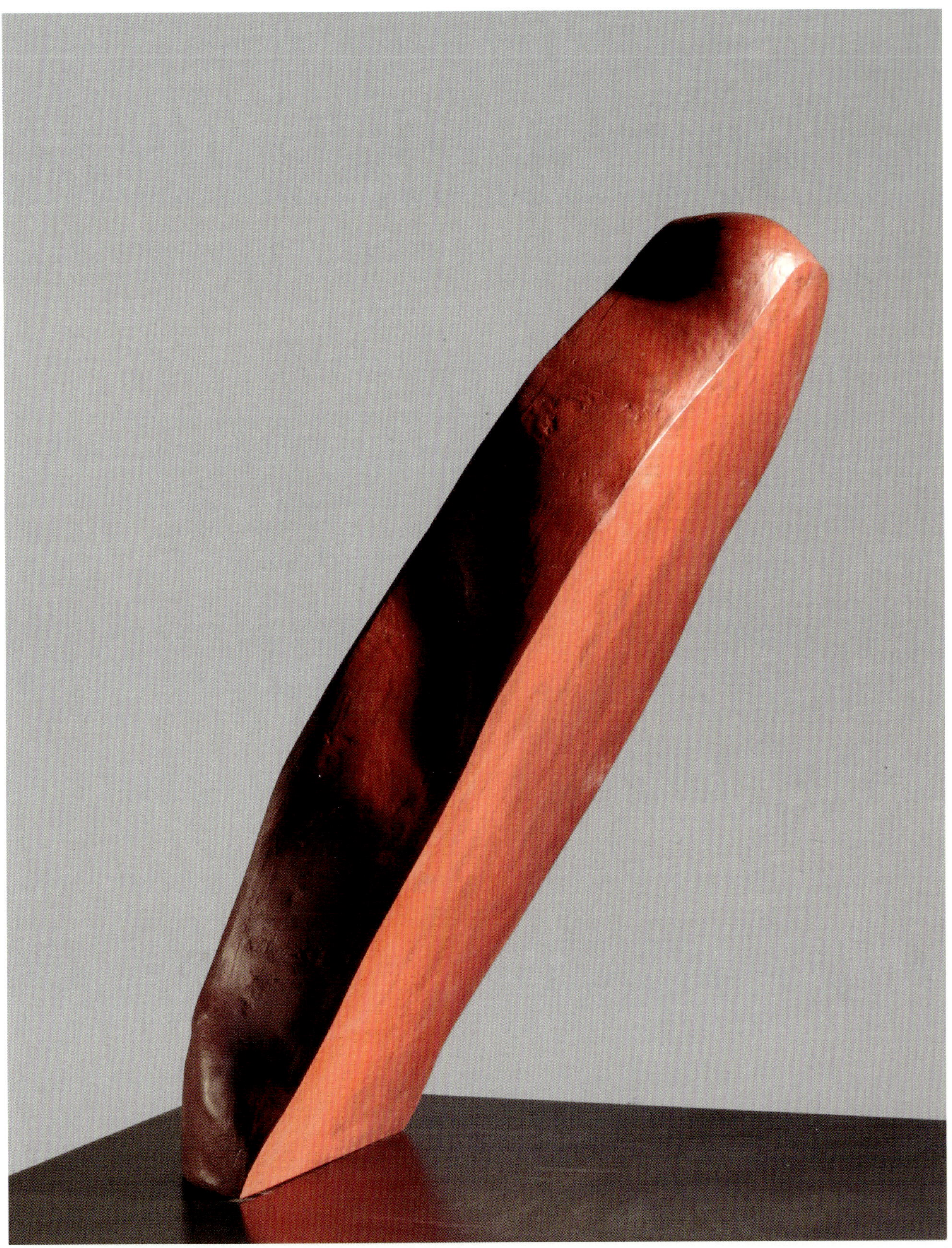

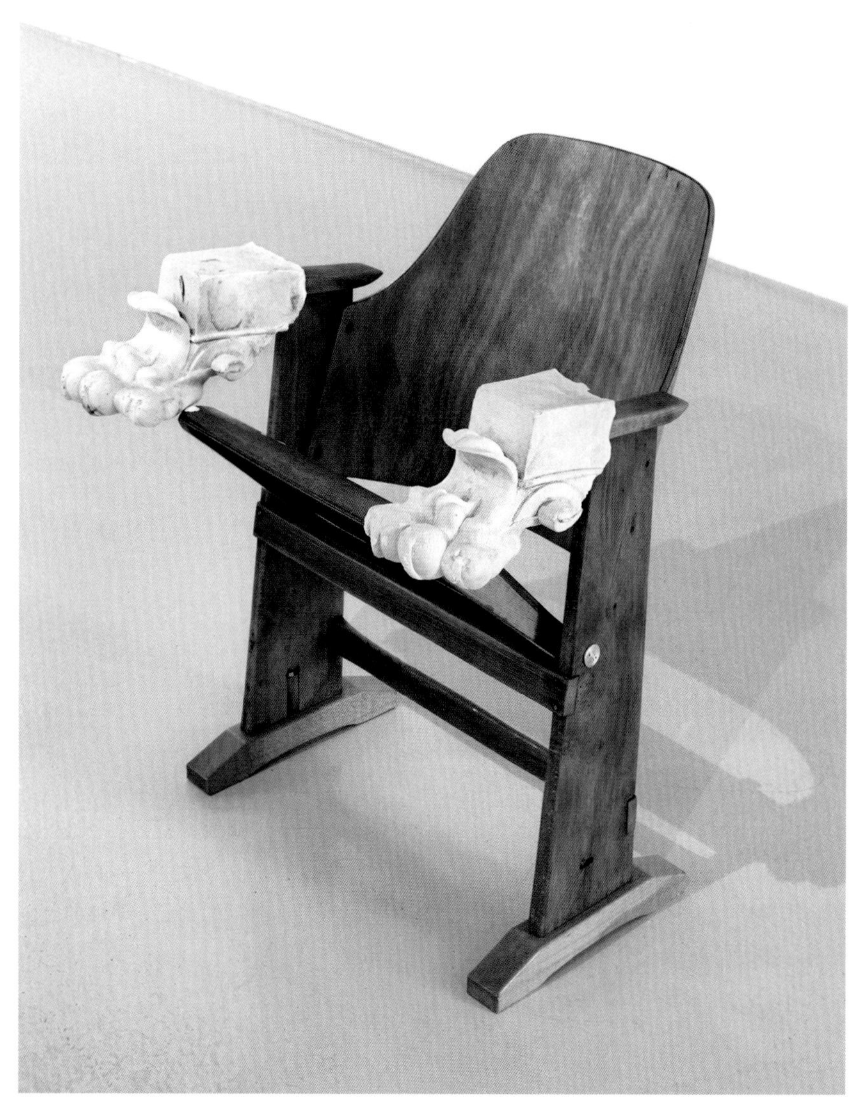

MONSTER, 2010
seating module, acrystal
79.5 x 59.5 x 64 cm

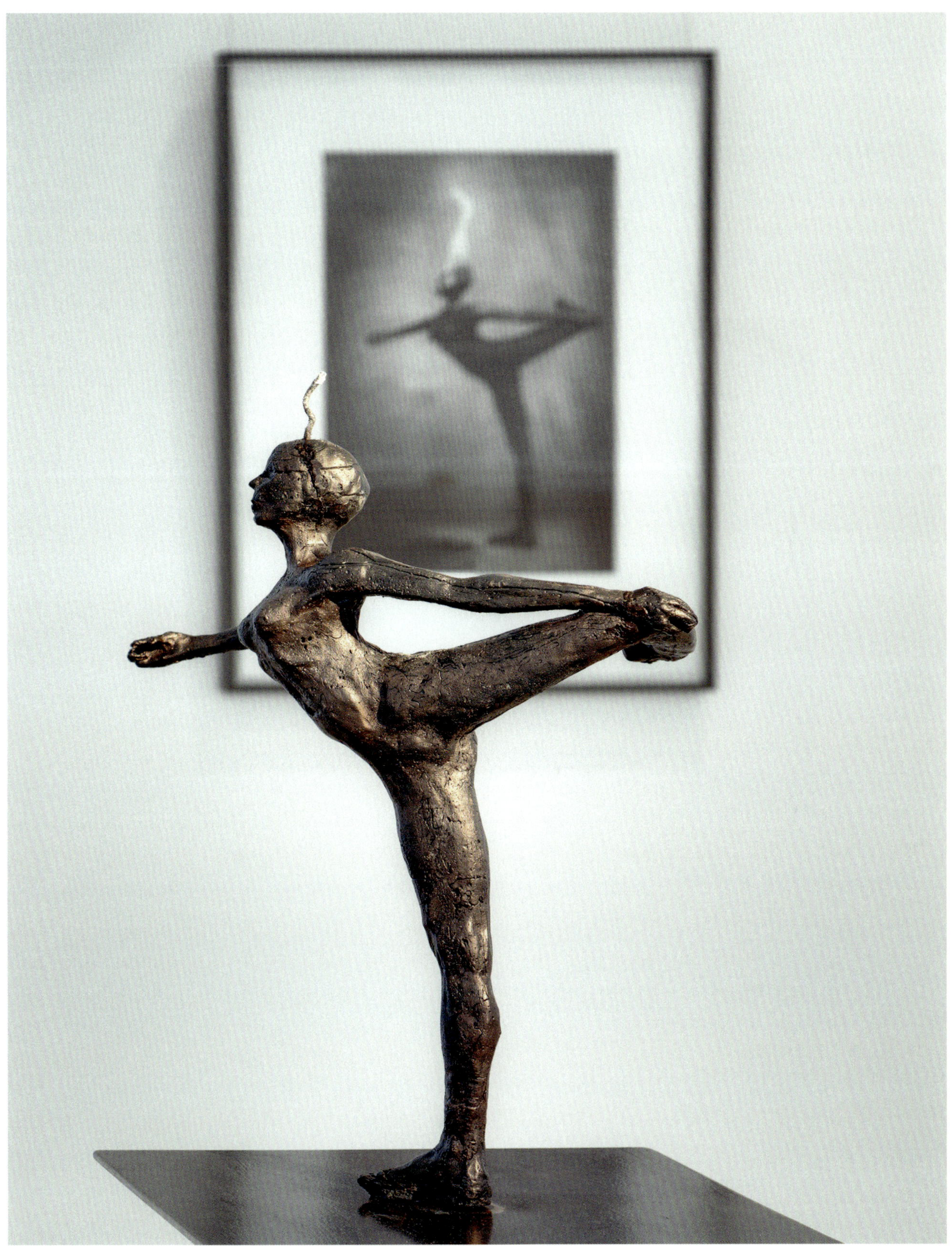

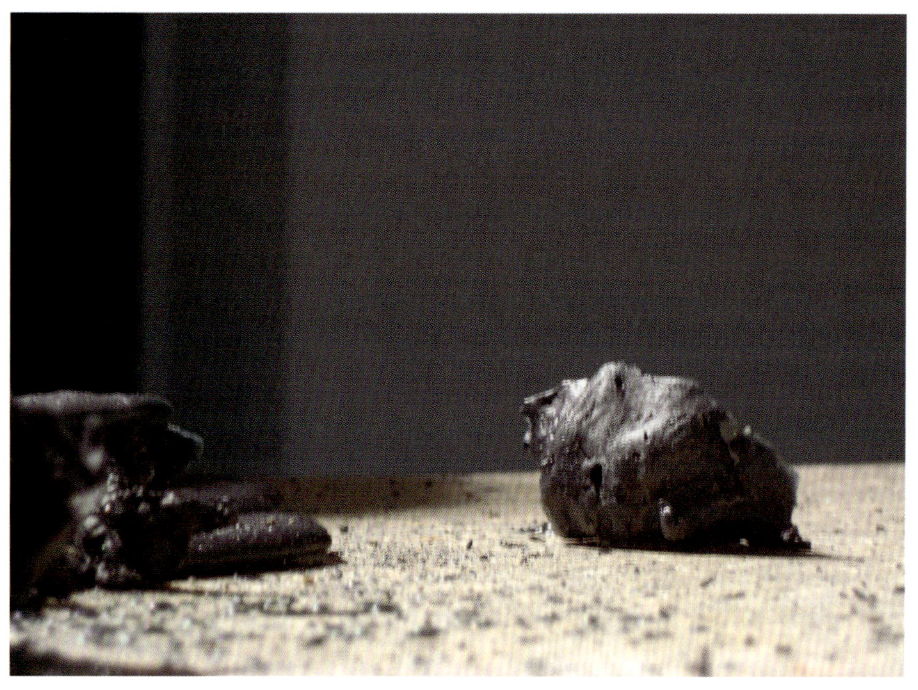

S. / pp. 21–23

DISARMING, 2009
photogravure on Buetten paper
89 x 66 cm, ed. of 15
and pigmented wax, wick
height 42 cm
Installation Turm Kunstverein Konstanz

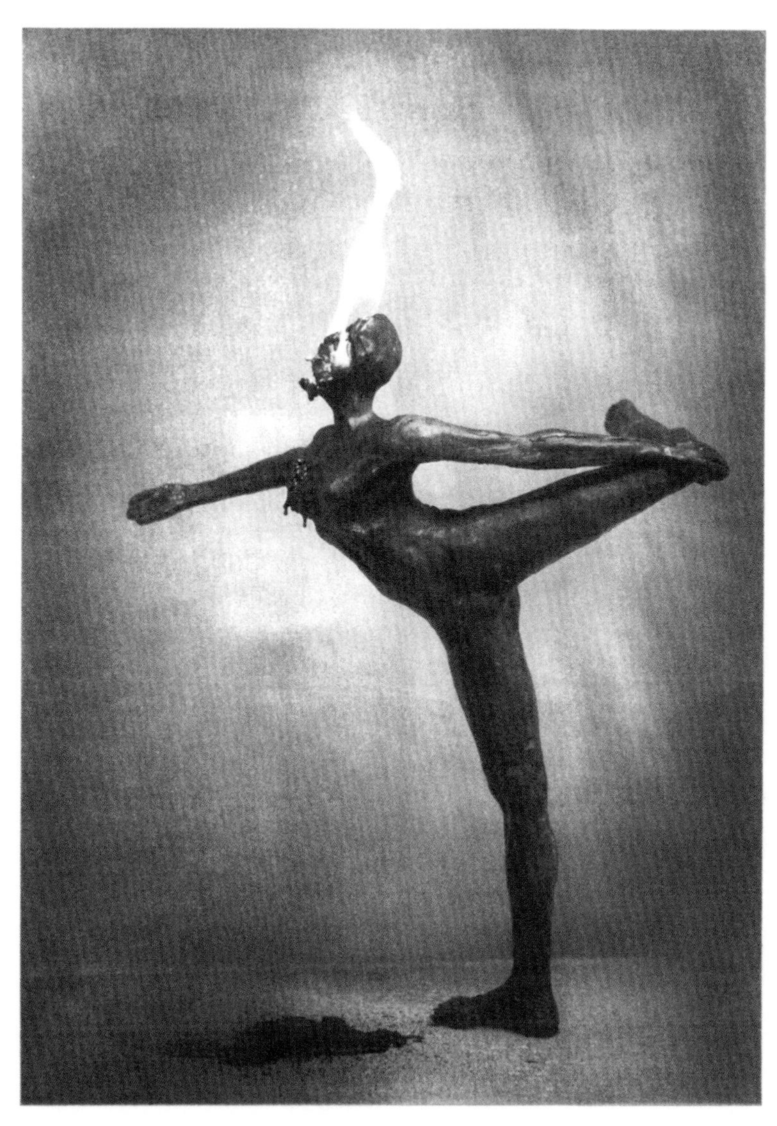

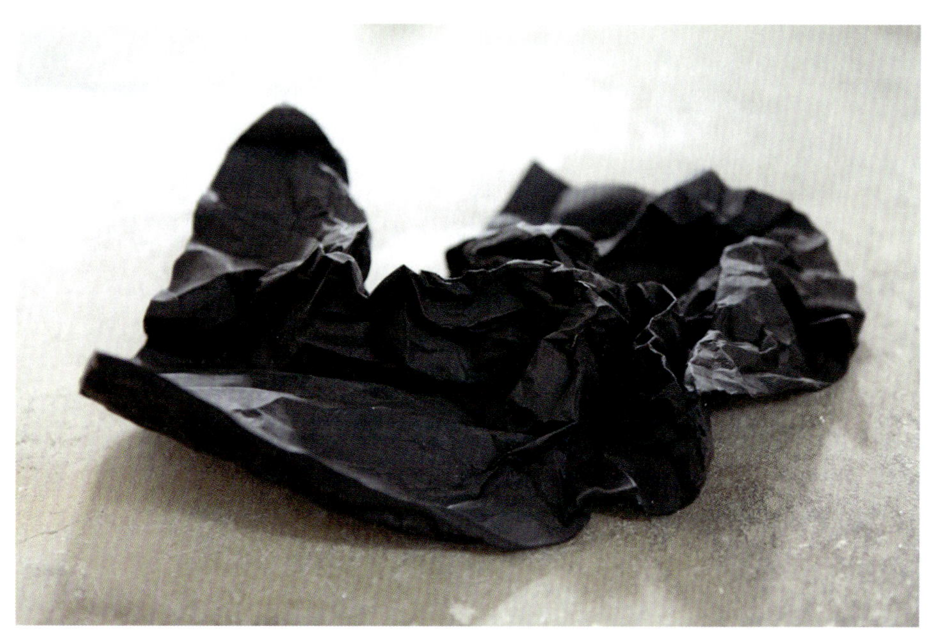

CRUMPLE (SCHIEF), 2013
patinized bronze
35 x 27 x 9 cm

ALLESDURCHDRINGUNG

Barbara Könches

Eine Flamme sticht gelb aus dem glühenden Schlund, greift sich einen Fetzen Papier. Schnell tanzt das weiße Blatt auf den spitzen Zungen der Flamme, zieht sich eilig zusammen, verkohlt, wird leicht und leichter. Dann im letzten Moment fliegt ein schwarz verrußter Fetzen schwerelos aus der bebenden Flamme, steigt zunächst in wirbelnder Drehbewegung in die Höhe, um anschließend wie auf gleitenden Schienen ganz allmählich und sehr langsam dem Boden entgegenzuschweben.

Schließlich liegt das verkohlte, verkrumpelte Blatt, oder besser das, was davon übrig bleibt, neben anderen ebenfalls versenkten Papierschnipseln. Jedes Einzelne bezieht seinen Ruheplatz im Raum so, als ob ein Choreograph es angewiesen hätte. Der Choreograph ist der Tanz-Schreiber, der in traditionellen und modernen Tanzaufführungen die Bewegungen der Tänzerinnen und Tänzer erfunden, einstudiert und als „seinen" Stil perfektioniert hat. Es gilt, durch Darstellung, Charaktere, Musik und Dramaturgie eine Geschichte zu erzählen. David Kishik verweist in seinem Essay „Das Tanz-Werk im Zeitalter des heiligen Lebens" darauf, dass der Choreograph nicht nur die Geschichten und die Geschichte eines oder des Tanzes aufzeichnet, sondern dass er vielmehr die enge Verwandtschaft von Tanz und Macht inkorporiert: „In der Tat betreten der moderne Staat und das ‚klassische' Ballett die Bühne der europäischen Geschichte zur selben Zeit. Es handelt sich hier jedoch nicht um eine Koinzidenz, sondern um Kausalität: obgleich die Menschen immer getanzt haben und immer tanzen werden, ist das Ballett ein legitimes Kind der modernen Politik."[1] Kishik argumentiert weiter, dass in der Zeit zwischen dem 16. und dem 20. Jahrhundert drei gängige Metaphern für den Tänzer bzw. die Tänzerin geläufig waren: zum einen der Vergleich mit einem Tier, zum anderen der Vergleich mit einer Maschine und schließlich: „Vom bereits erwähnten Begriff des *corps de ballet* bis zu jenem ikonischen Augenblick des Balletts, in dem der hinter der Ballerina stehende Tänzer deren Körper anhebt und dem souveränen Auge des Zuschauers darbietet, erweist sich das Ballett als ein biopolitisches Theater, wie es perfekter nicht sein könnte."[2]

Erst die Künstlerinnen und Künstler in New York Anfang der 1960er-Jahre haben die Fesseln des disziplinierten, reglementierten Körpers gesprengt, indem sie selbst das Wagnis eingegangen sind, ihrer Arbeit neue Paradigmen zu unterstellen. Es waren die Tänzerinnen und Tänzer im Umfeld des Judson Church Theatres, die ihre künstlerische Tätigkeit nicht länger in der Aufführung eines choreographierten dramaturgischen Auftritts sahen, sondern vielmehr im spielerischen Prozess alltägliche Bewegungen auf die Bühne brachten. Zufall und algorithmische Handlungsanweisungen spielten dabei eine ebenso große Rolle wie die individuellen Bewegungen der einzelnen Tänzerinnen und Tänzer bzw. Performer. Die Durchlässigkeit, die Grenzüberschreitungen und die Kooperationen zwischen Musikern wie John Cage, Tänzern wie Merce Cunnigham, Malern wie Robert Rauschenberg oder Jasper Johns beeinflussten die Gruppe junger Künstlerinnen und Künstler wie Yvonne Rainer, Robert Morris, Trisha Brown, die in der Judson Church probten und auftraten.

Der Choreograph oder die Choreographin verändert seine oder ihre Praxis hin zum „Lese-Schreiber". Er oder sie versucht, wie ein Seismograph die Bewegungen im Raum aufzuzeichnen, auszuwerten und an die Umwelt zurückzusenden. „Diese Modi des Schreibens", so resümiert Gabriele Brandstetter, „das sich an ein Lesen knüpft, zeichnen nicht nur ein choreographisches Konzept, sondern sie strukturieren zugleich die Inszenierung des (Kompositions-)Konzepts. Die Performance selbst organisiert sich als Schreibpraxis, d. h., es findet hier nicht etwa eine räumlich skripturale oder graphische Umsetzung von (vorher) geschriebenen Regeln statt ..."[3]

Beim Durchblättern des Entwurfs für diesen Katalog von Maren Maurer fühle ich mich an die historische Entwicklung des Tanzes erinnert. Zunächst sicherlich ausgehend von dem Wissen, dass sie selbst Tänzerin werden wollte, bevor sie bildende Kunst studierte. Die Auseinandersetzung mit dem Ballett, mit Tanz und Bewegung nimmt eine zentrale Stellung in ihrem noch jungen und im Wachsen begriffenen Werk ein. Wenn die wächserne Tänzerin „disarming“ in der Pose „Attitude“ (frz.) [Seite 21–23] lichterloh brennt, so befindet sie sich in einem Prozess der Metamorphose, der Gestaltumwandlung, die zunächst die strenge Körperdisziplinierung zerstört, auflöst und Energie und Materie gleichermaßen freisetzt, um neue Formen der Akkumulation zu ermöglichen. Körper entgrenzen sich und treten in neue Bezüge zueinander und zu dem sie umgebenden Raum. Die hierarchisch strenge Choreographie, das Einschreiben von Disziplin und Machtgefüge wird hier wie in der Judson Church außer Kraft gesetzt auf der Suche nach einer ausgeglichenen und doch nicht willkürlichen neuen Raumordnung. Ich sehe diese Art der Choreographie in verschiedenen Arbeiten wie „Ach, jetzt habe ich es vergessen“ [Seite 36–37] oder „wir teilen“ [Seite 32–33] ins Werk gesetzt. Die einzelnen Exponate im Raum erinnern an ein verkohltes Papier, an ein zerknülltes Notizblatt oder an verdorrte Äste und Pflanzenblätter, wie in der Arbeit „Raute“ [Seite 90]. Sobald jedoch ein zweites und drittes Exponat dazukommt, befindet sich die Gruppe in einem Prozess der Zuordnung – sowohl untereinander als auch in Bezug auf den sie umgebenen Raum. Mir erscheint dieser Aspekt ganz wesentlich: dass die Summe der einzelnen sich vermeintlich in Auflösung und Transformation befindlichen Stücke keinesfalls die Ansammlung von erschöpfter Materie darstellt, sondern die Teile aus der als beliebig erscheinenden Anordnung eine neue Struktur entwickeln, die ihnen eine andere Attraktivität verleiht und die Gruppe insgesamt in eine neue Form der harmonischen Koexistenz überführt.

„Hic sunt dracones“, so erklärte mir Maren, sind die unbekannten Gebiete auf der Landkarte, die vielleicht auch besser nicht betreten werden sollten, denn dort leben die Drachen. Dieses Fabeltier wird gleichzeitig gefürchtet und geliebt, da es wie Prometheus die Gewalt über das Feuer ausübt und aus dem Chaos eine neue Ordnung errichtet.

[1] David Kishik, „Das Tanz-Werk im Zeitalter des heiligen Lebens“, in: Allesdurchdringung, Berlin 2008, S. 45–60, S. 49.
[2] Ebd., S. 51.
[3] Gabriele Brandstetter, „Bild-Sprung“, o.O. 2005, S. 64. [Theater der Zeit, Recherchen 26]

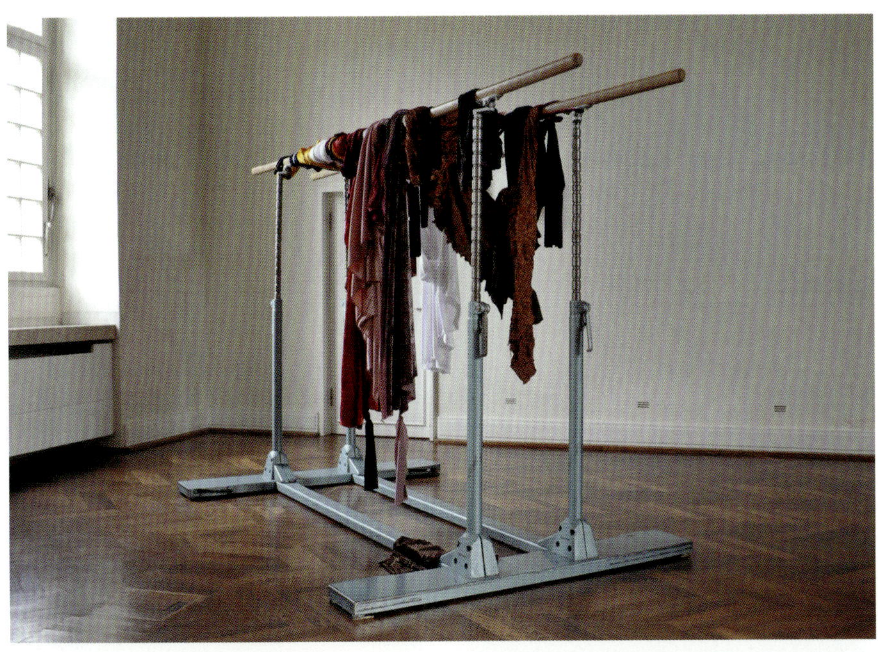

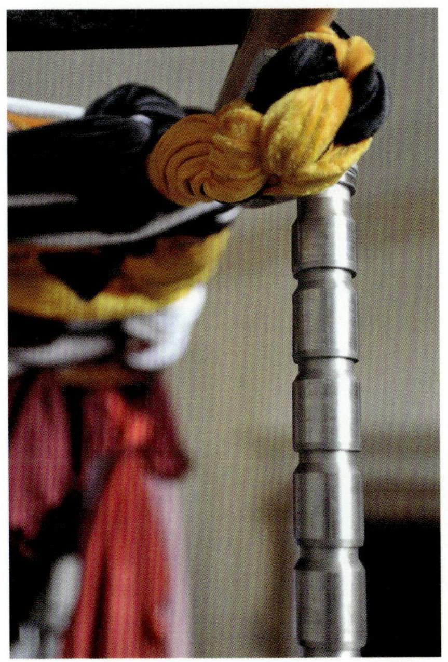

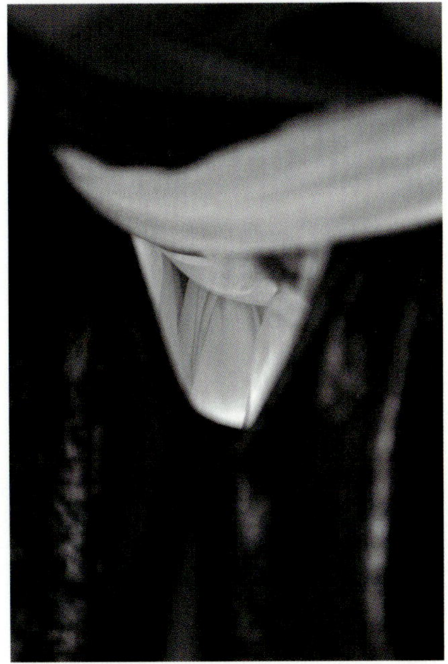

I PUT MY HEAD INTO AN OCEAN, 2008
parallel bars, cloth
350 x 180 x 164 cm
Installation Schloss Benrath

ALL-PERVASION

Barbara Könches

A yellow flame darts out of the smoldering maw, grabbing a shred of paper. The white piece of paper dances on the flame's pointed tongues, contracts rapidly, burns to a cinder, becomes lighter and lighter. Finally, a black, sooty flake hovers weightlessly above the quivering flame; it rises up high in whirling circles before floating towards the floor gently and slowly, as though moving on sliding rails.

Finally, the charred, crumpled piece of paper – or what's left of it – lies on the floor, next to other, equally scorched snippets. Every single one takes its place on the floor as though it had been allotted to it by a choreographer in advance. A choreographer is a writer of dance, who has invented, studied and perfected "his" style of instructing the movements of dancers in traditional and modern dance performances. The aim is to tell a story through performance, characters, music and dramaturgy. In his essay "The Work of Dance in the Age of Sacred Lives," David Kishik points out that the choreographer does not merely record the stories and the history of dance or a dance, but rather incorporates the close relationship between dance and power: "The modern state and 'classical' ballet do indeed enter the stage of European history at the same time. This, however, is not a coincidence, but in fact constitutes a causality: even though people have always danced and will always dance, ballet is a legitimate child of modern politics."[1] Kishik further argues that three popular metaphors were commonly used to describe a dancer in the period between the 16th and 20th centuries. These were firstly the comparison with an animal, secondly, dancers were compared to machines, and finally: "From the previously mentioned term *corps de ballet* to that iconic moment during ballet performances in which the male dancer standing behind the ballerina lifts her body up and presents it to the sovereign eye of the viewer, ballet proves itself to be bio-political theatre of the most perfect kind."[2]

It was the New York artists of the early 1960s who broke the shackles of the disciplined, regimented body by daring to assume new paradigms for their work. The dancers in the sphere of the Judson Dance Theater group no longer considered their artistic work to lie in performing a choreographed theatrical piece. Instead, they brought everyday movements to the stage in a playful process. Chance and algorithmic instructions for movement played a significant role in this, as did the individual movements of single dancers or performers. Permeability, the transcending of borders and cooperation among musicians such as John Cage, dancers such as Merce Cunningham and painters such as Robert Rauschenberg or Jasper Johns influenced the group of young artists who rehearsed and performed in Judson Church, including Yvonne Rainer, Robert Morris and Trisha Brown.

The choreographer changes his/her practice, becoming a "reader-writer." Like a seismograph, he/she seeks to record and analyze the movements in the space and send them back out into the environment. "These modes of writing," summarizes Gabriele Brandstetter, "which are connected to a reading, not only sketch out a choreographic concept, but also structure the orchestration of a (compositional) concept. The performance itself if then organized as a writing practice, meaning, this is no spatially scriptural or graphic implementation of (previously) written rules ..."[3]

Flicking through the draft for this catalog by Maren Maurer, I find myself reminded of the historical development of dance. This may indeed be based on my knowledge of the fact that she wanted to be a dancer before deciding to study fine art. The exploration of ballet, dance and movement has a central place in her still young and growing oeuvre. When the waxen dancer in her piece "disarming" in the pose "Attitude" (Fr.) [page 21–23] is set ablaze, she is in a process of metamorphosis, of shape-shifting, that first destroys and dissolves the strict disciplining of the body – setting free both energy and material in equal measure – in order to enable new forms of accumulation. Bodies merge and enter into new relationships

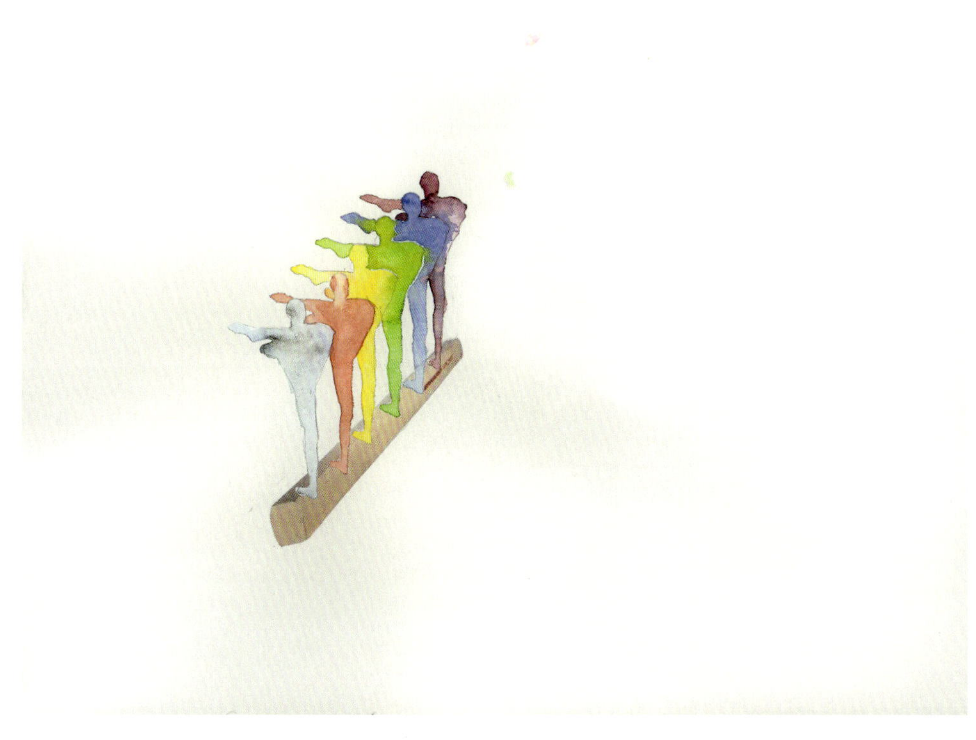

NO TITLE, 2009
watercolor, collage
37,6 x 49,4 cm

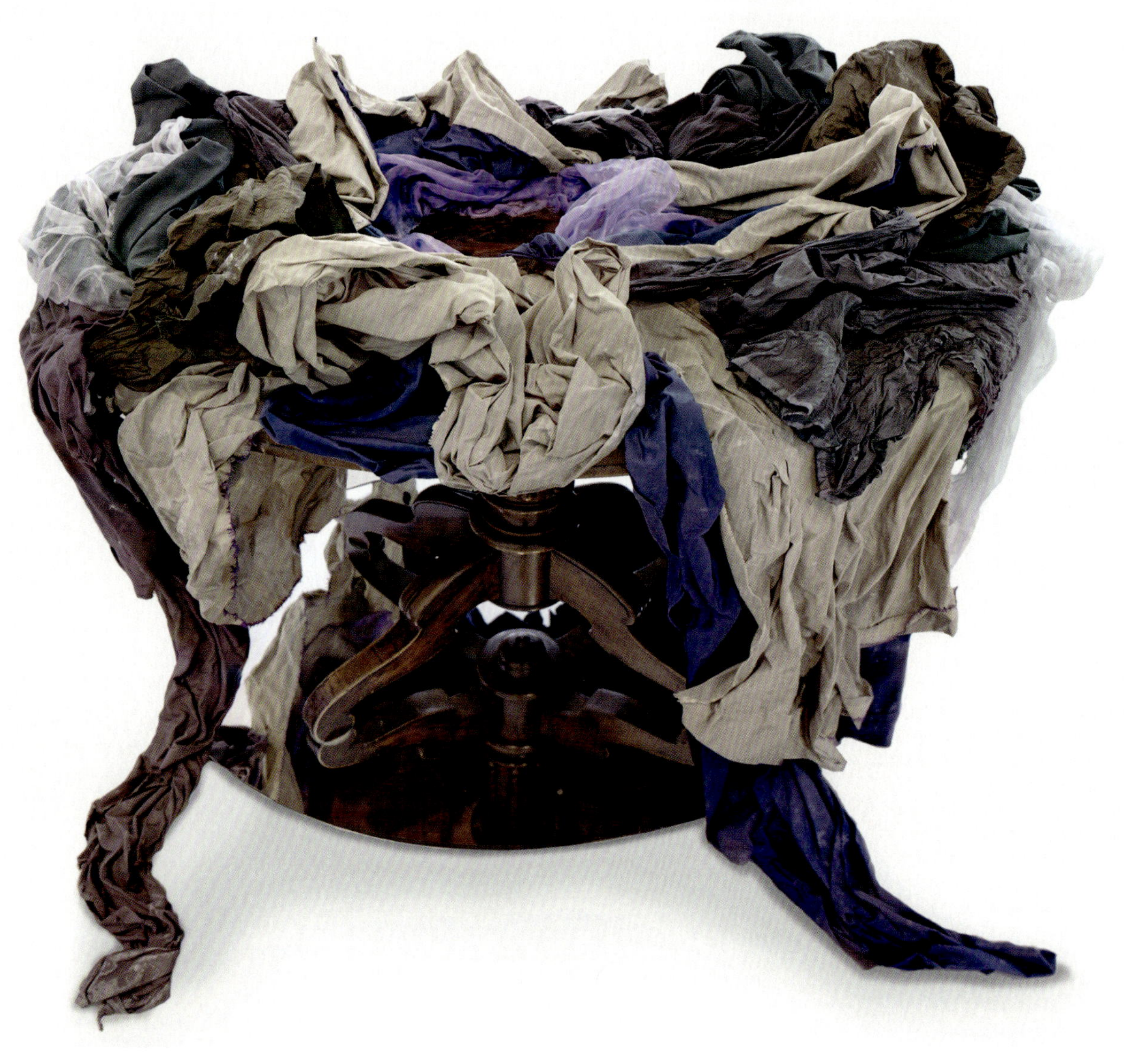

PRESENT OF REALITY, 2009
table, mirror, stiffed cloth
140 x 100 x 100 cm

with one another and the space surrounding them. The strict hierarchical choreography, the inscribing of discipline and power relations are overridden here, as they were in Judson Church, in the search for a balanced yet not arbitrary restructuring of space. I see this kind of choreography implemented in various works, such as "Ach, jetzt habe ich es vergessen" [page 36/37] or "wir teilen" [page 32–33]. The individual exhibits in the gallery space are reminiscent of charred paper, a crumpled-up page from a notebook or dry branches and plant leaves, as is the case in the piece entitled "Raute" [page 90]. Yet as soon as a second or third exhibit is added, the group enters a process of correlation – both among the individual works and in relation to the space surrounding them. I see this as a crucial aspect, the fact that the sum of the parts, which by themselves are presumably in a state of dissolution or transformation, by no means constitutes a collection of depleted material. Rather, in their seemingly random arrangement these parts start to form a new structure that lends them a different appeal, turning the group as a whole into a new form of harmonious coexistence.

"Hic sunt dracones," as Maren explains to me, are those uncharted regions on a map that we would be wise not to seek out, as this is where dragons live. This mythical creature is both loved and feared, as, like Prometheus, it has power over fire and creates a new order from chaos.

[1] *David Kishik, "Das Tanz-Werk im Zeitalter des heiligen Lebens," in: Allesdurchdringung, Berlin 2008, pp. 45–60, here p. 49 (quotations have been translated from the German).*
[2] *Ibid., p. 51.*
[3] *Gabriele Brandstetter, "Bild-Sprung", no place of publication given, 2005, p. 64. [Theater der Zeit, Recherchen 26]*

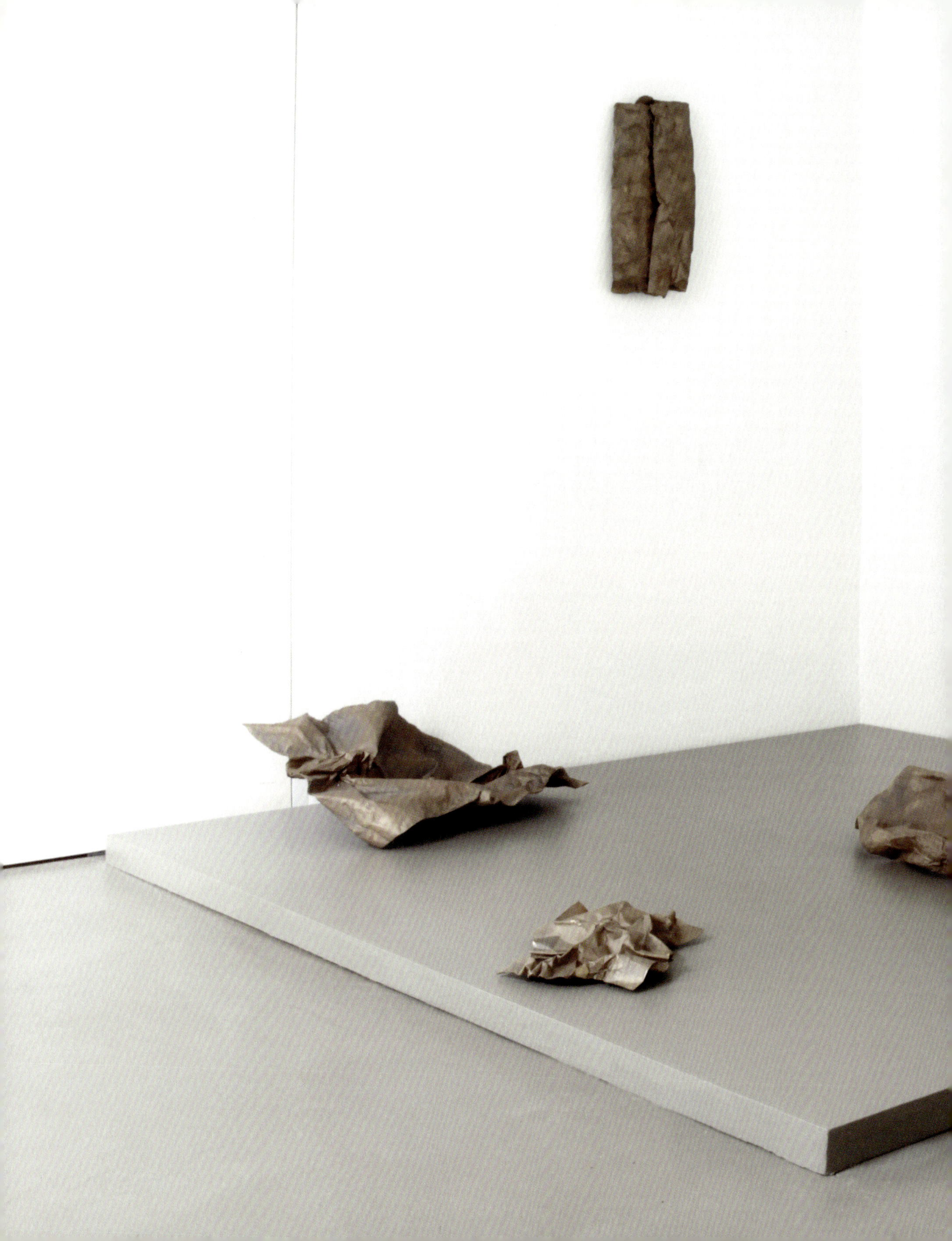

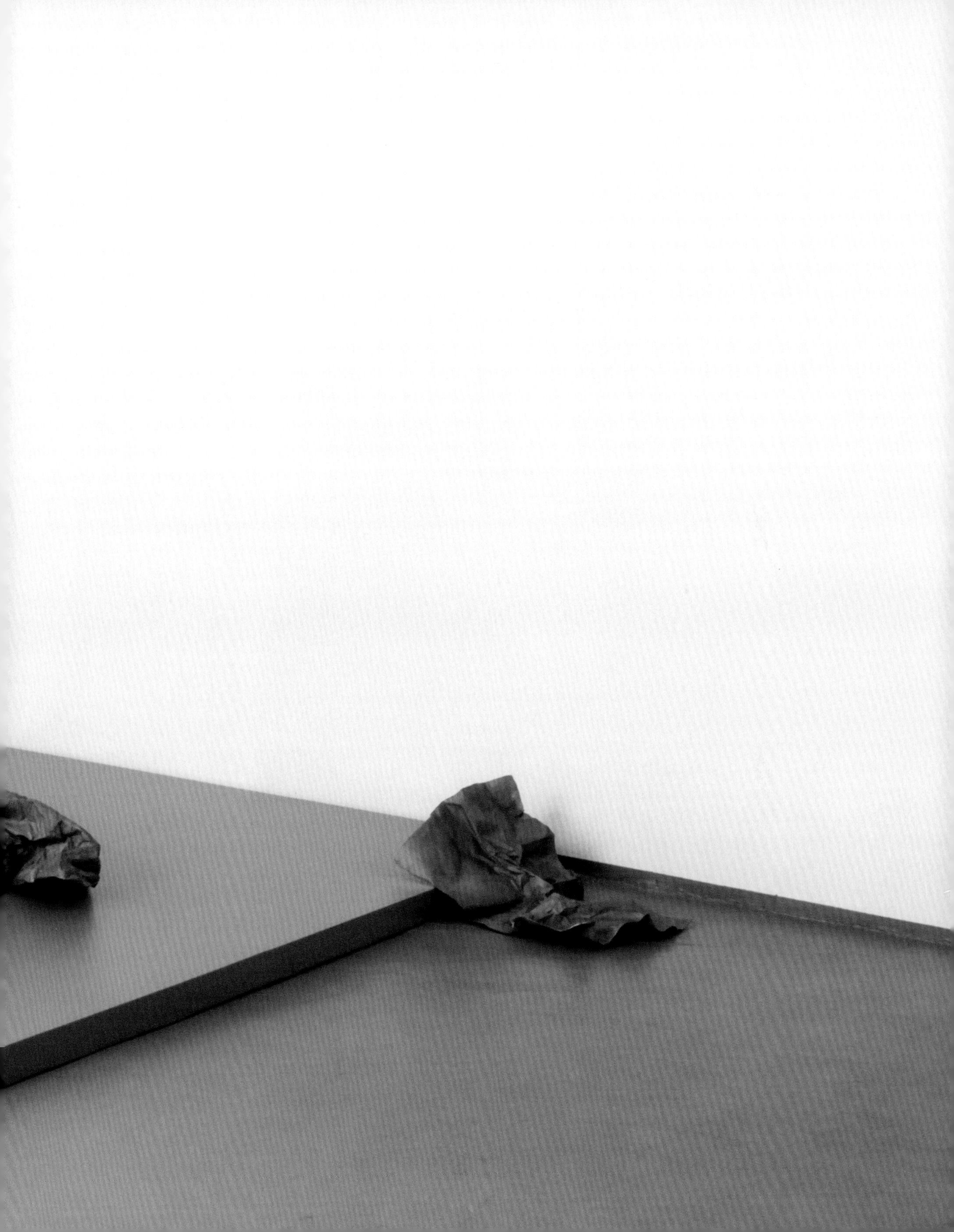

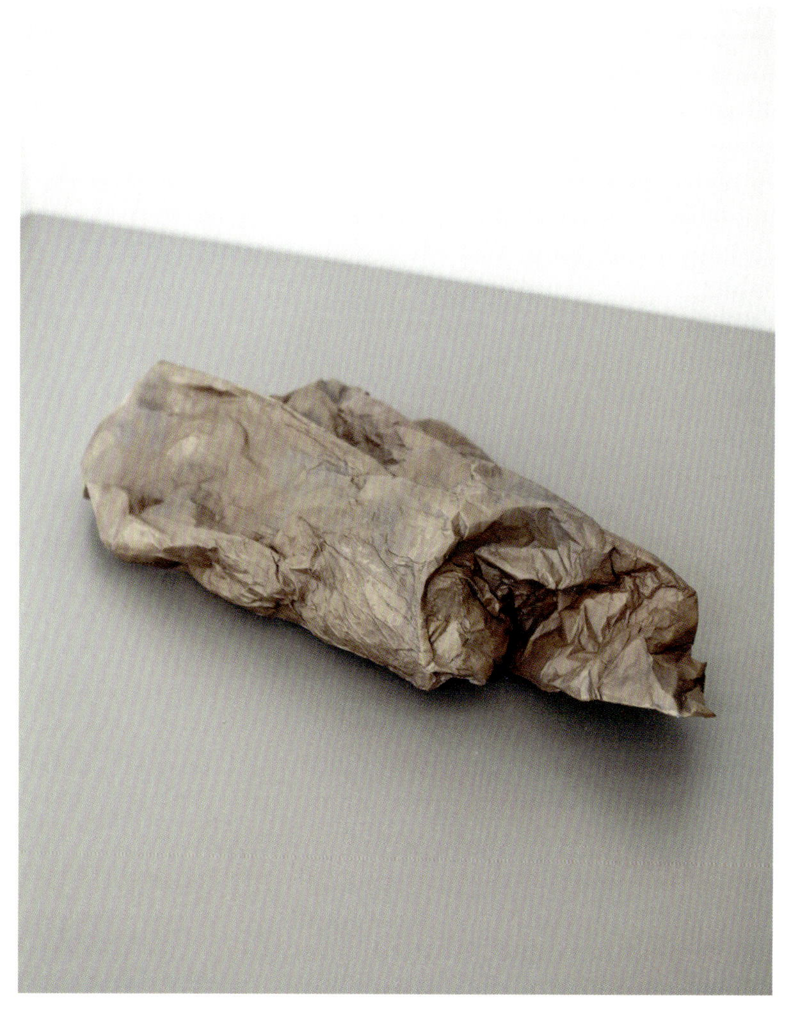

S. / pp. 32–35

WIR TEILEN, 2014
bronze, various formats,
20.03.2014 'Breathe Normally'
Installation RAUM Oberkassel

S. / p. 34

CRUMPLE (TUNNEL), 2014
bronze, 85 x 47 cm

S. / p. 35

CRUMPLE (KLEINE ECKE), 2014
bronze, 49 x 33 cm

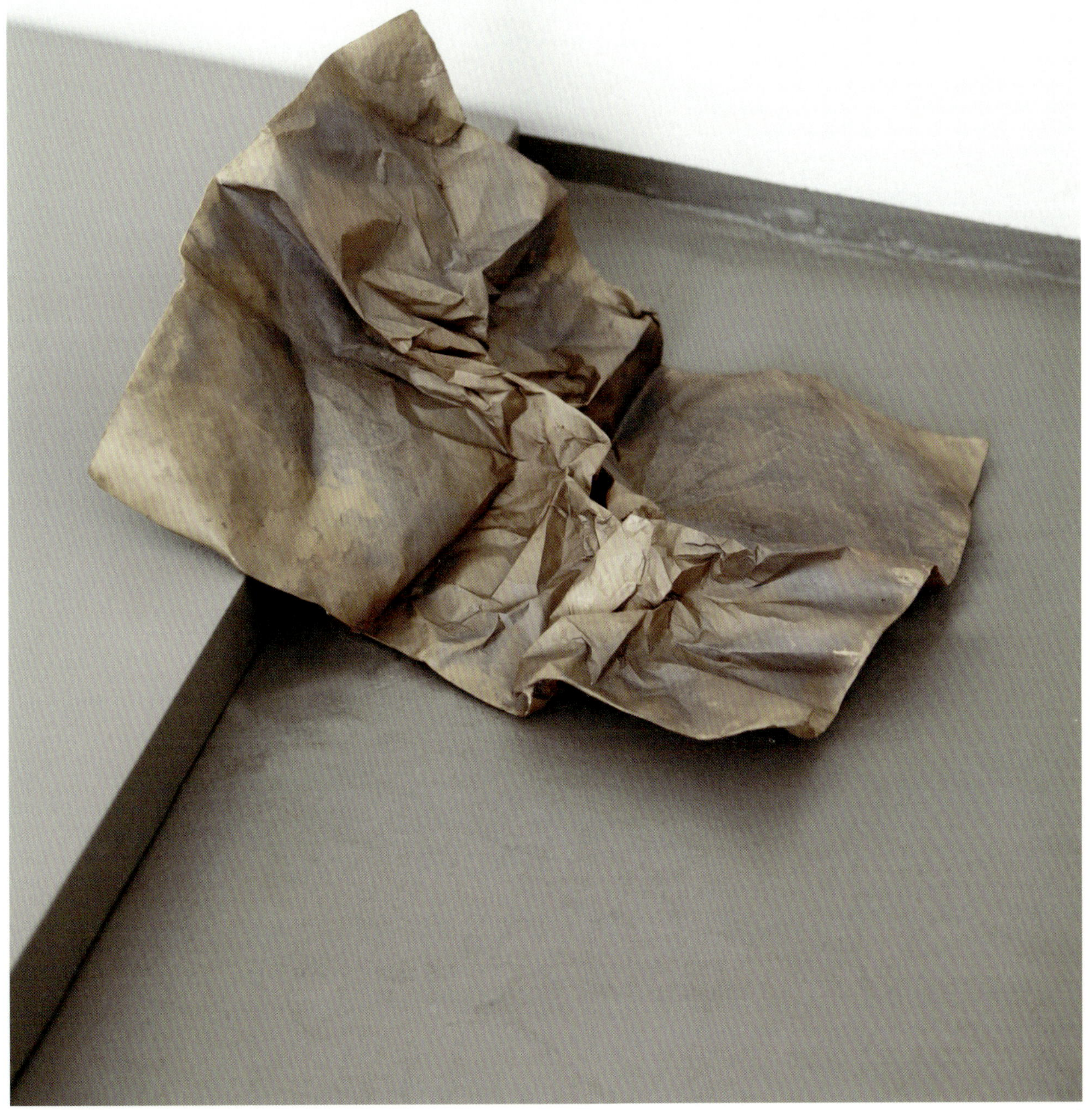

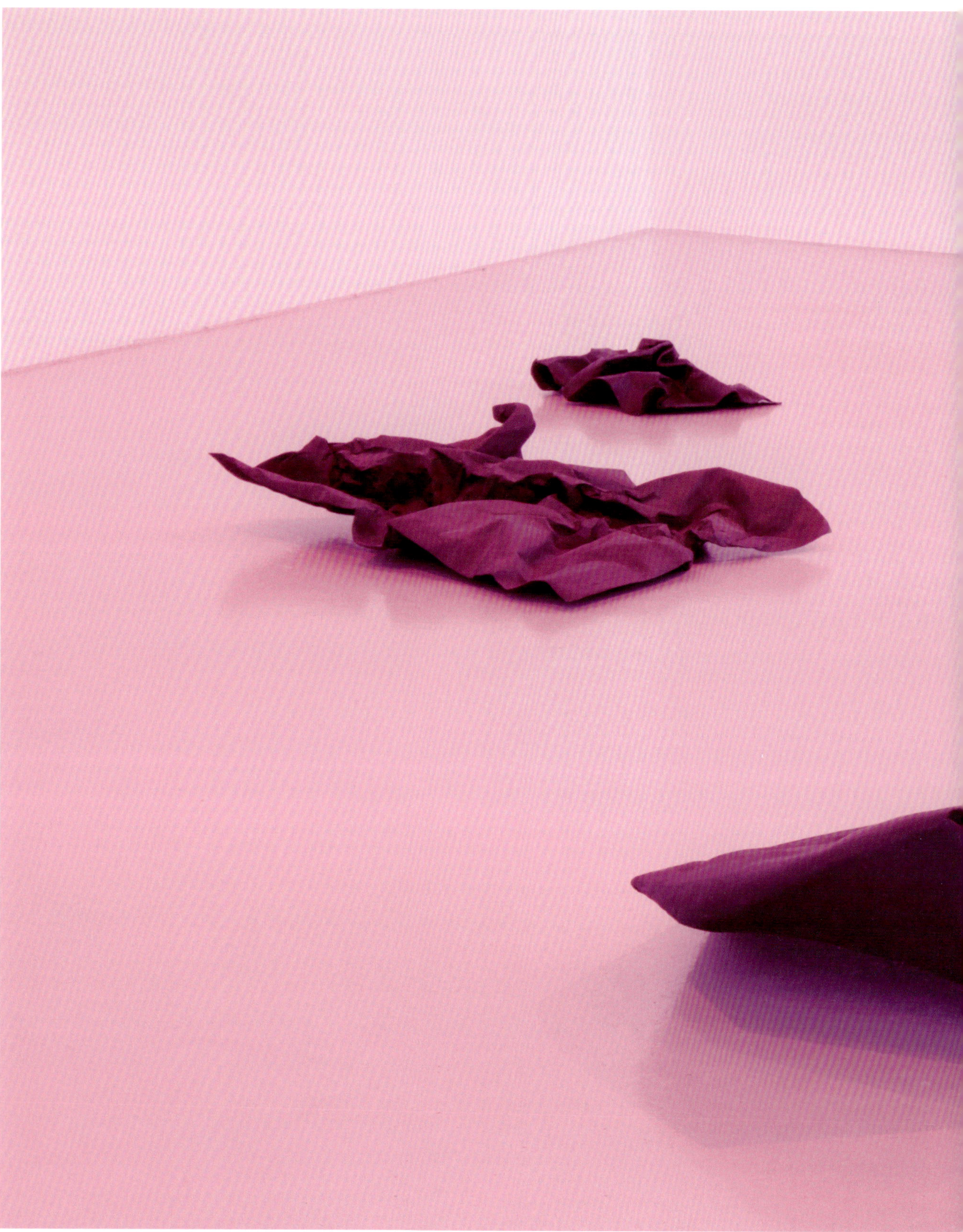

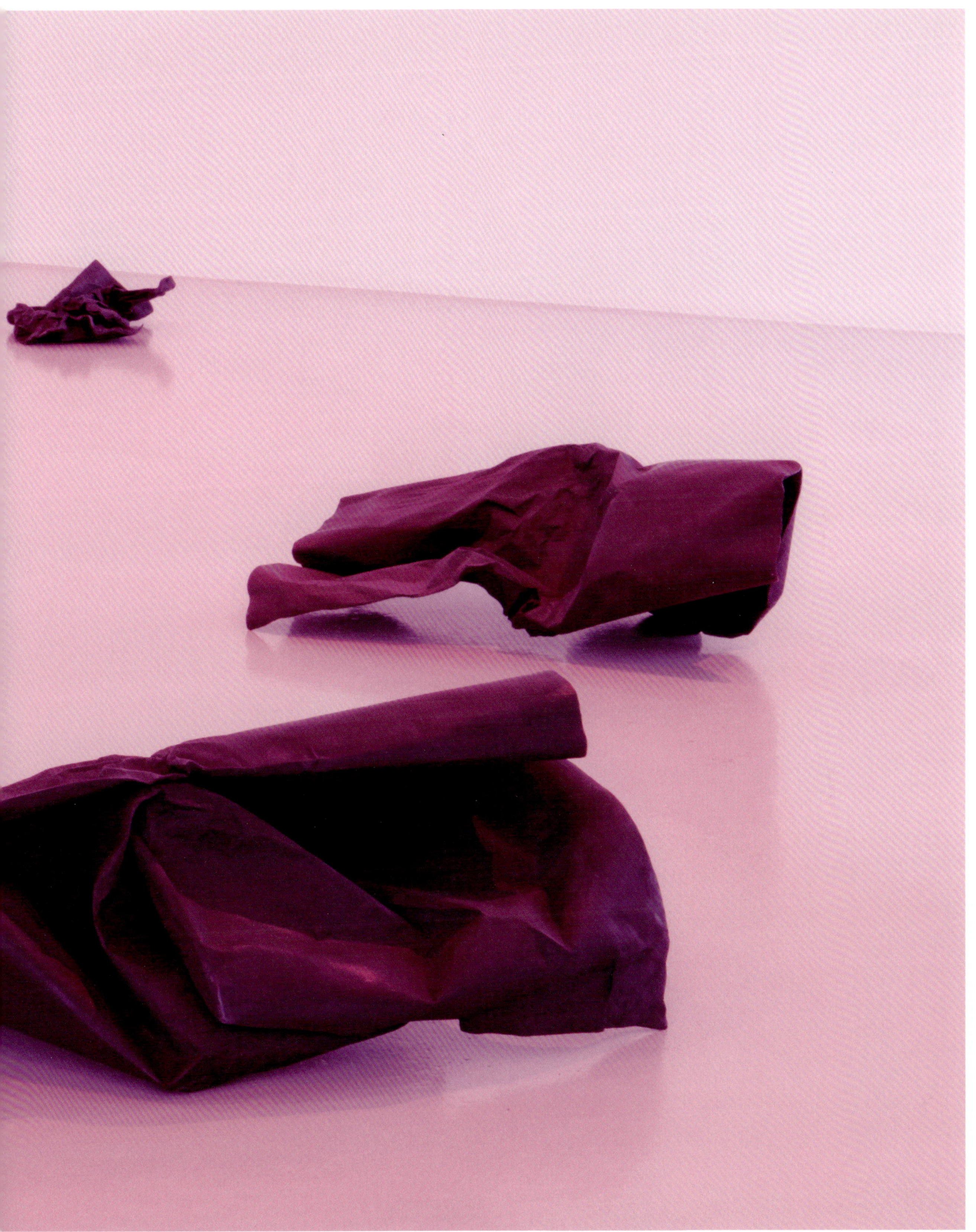

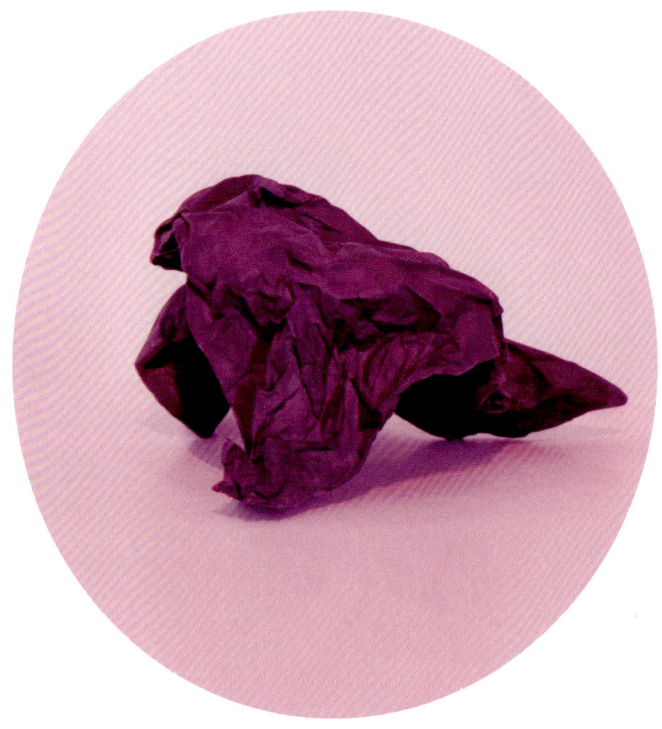

S. / pp. 36–37

ACH, JETZT HABE ICH ES VERGESSEN, 2014
magenta light, patinized bronze, various formats
Installation Turm Kunstverein Konstanz

S. / p. 38

CRUMPLE (KRAKE), 2014
bronze on pedestal, 26 x 21 x 12 cm

S. / p. 39

CRUMPLE (MR. VAN AND FRIENDS), 2014
patinized bronze, 70 x 28 cm

S. / pp. 41–45

CHAKRAPENG!, 2015
duration 150 min
Performance Kai 10
18.04.2015 'Broken Spaces'

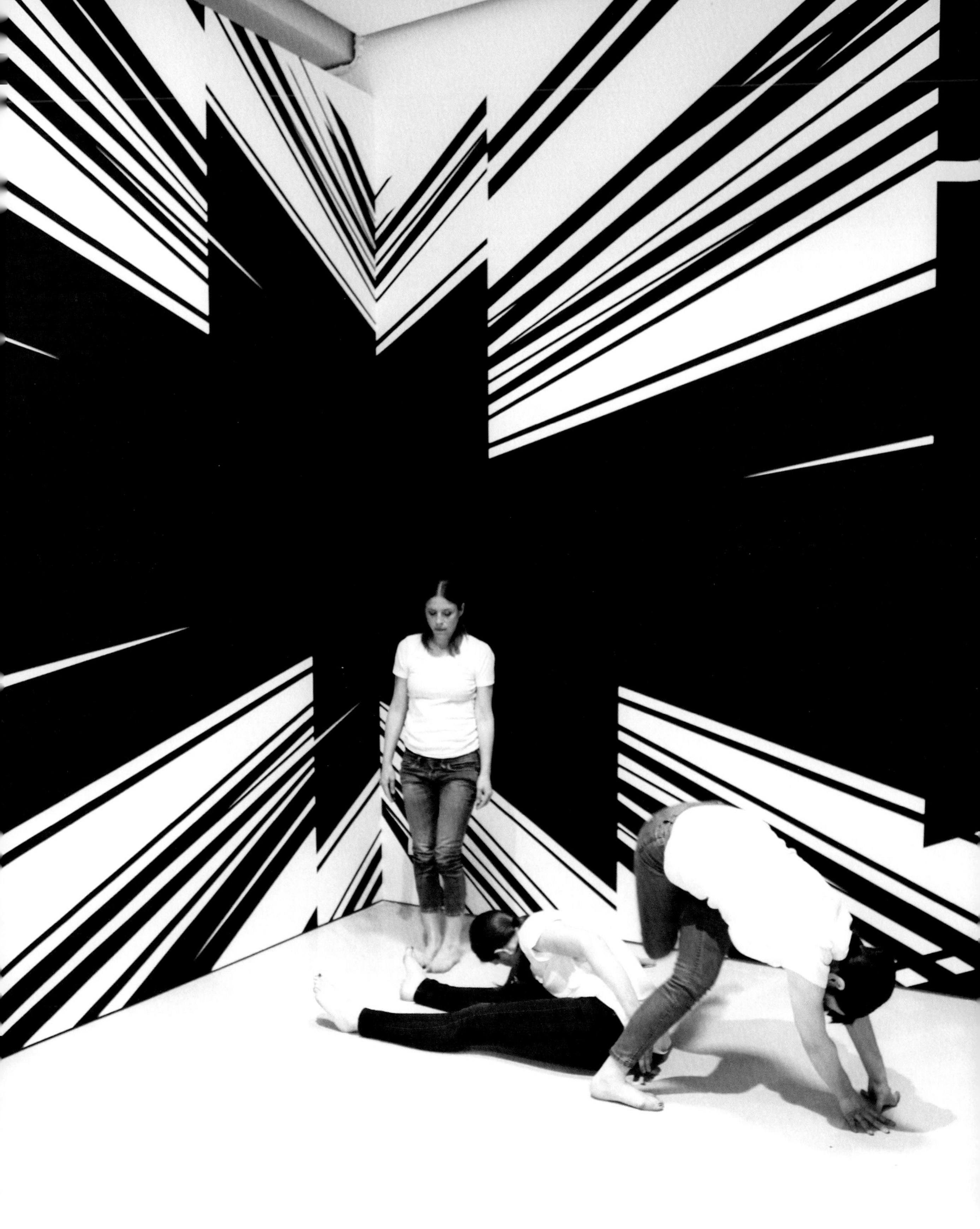

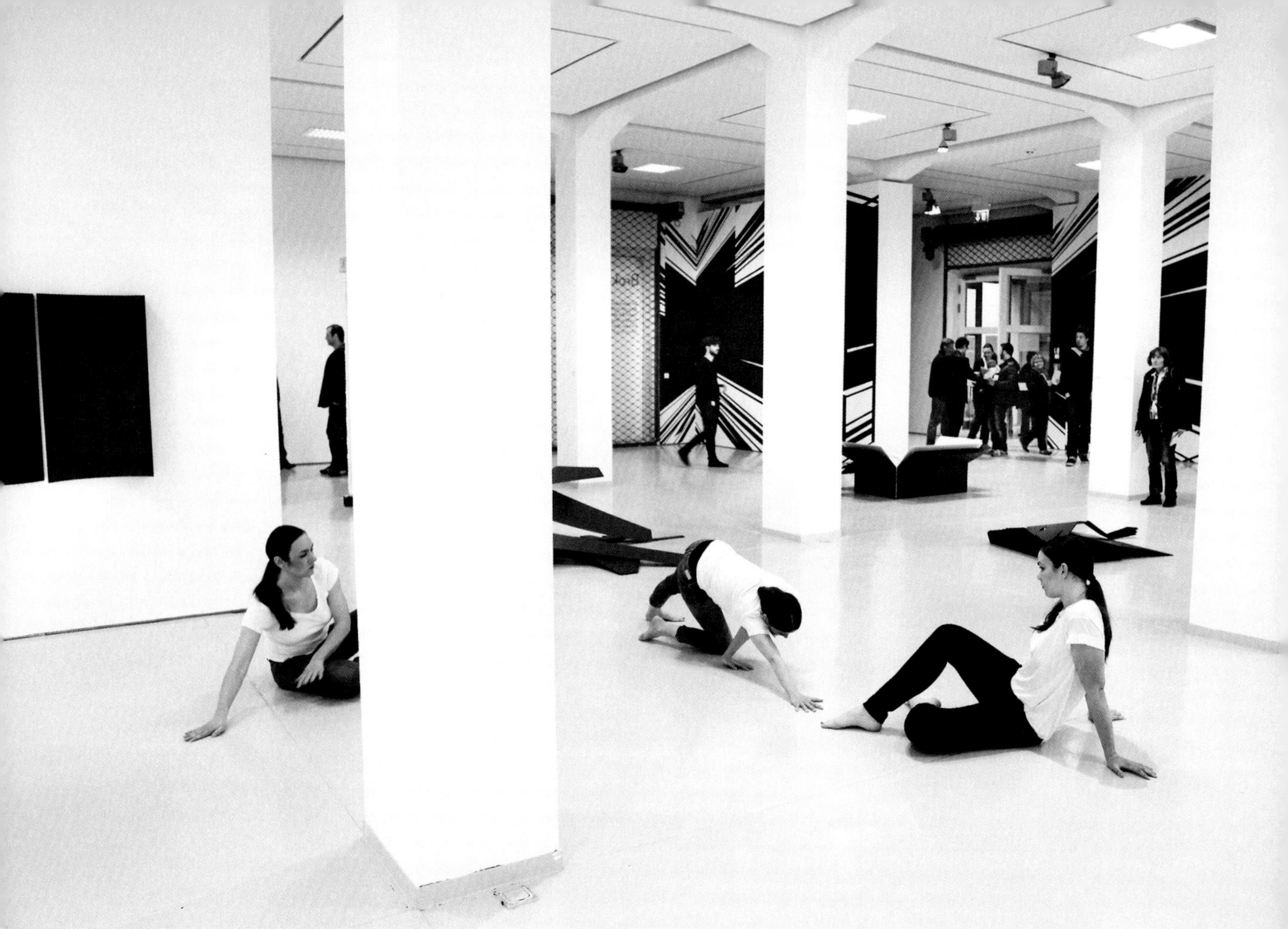

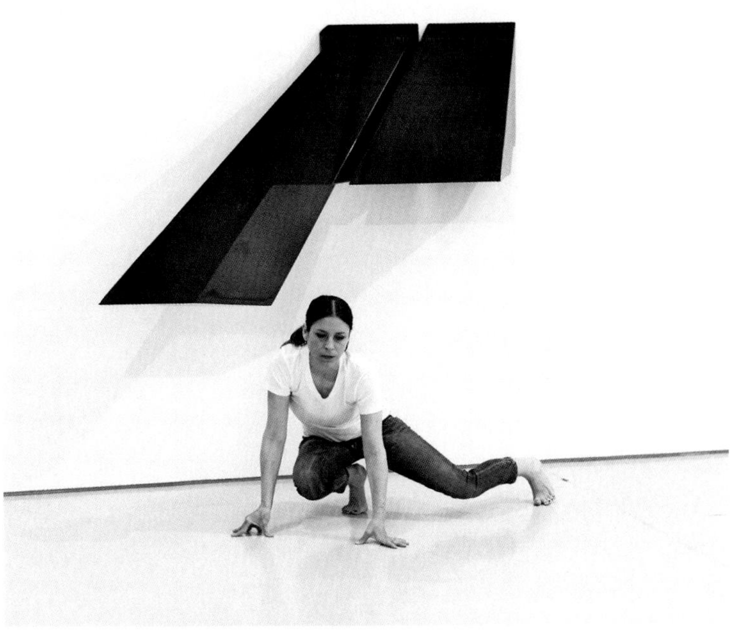

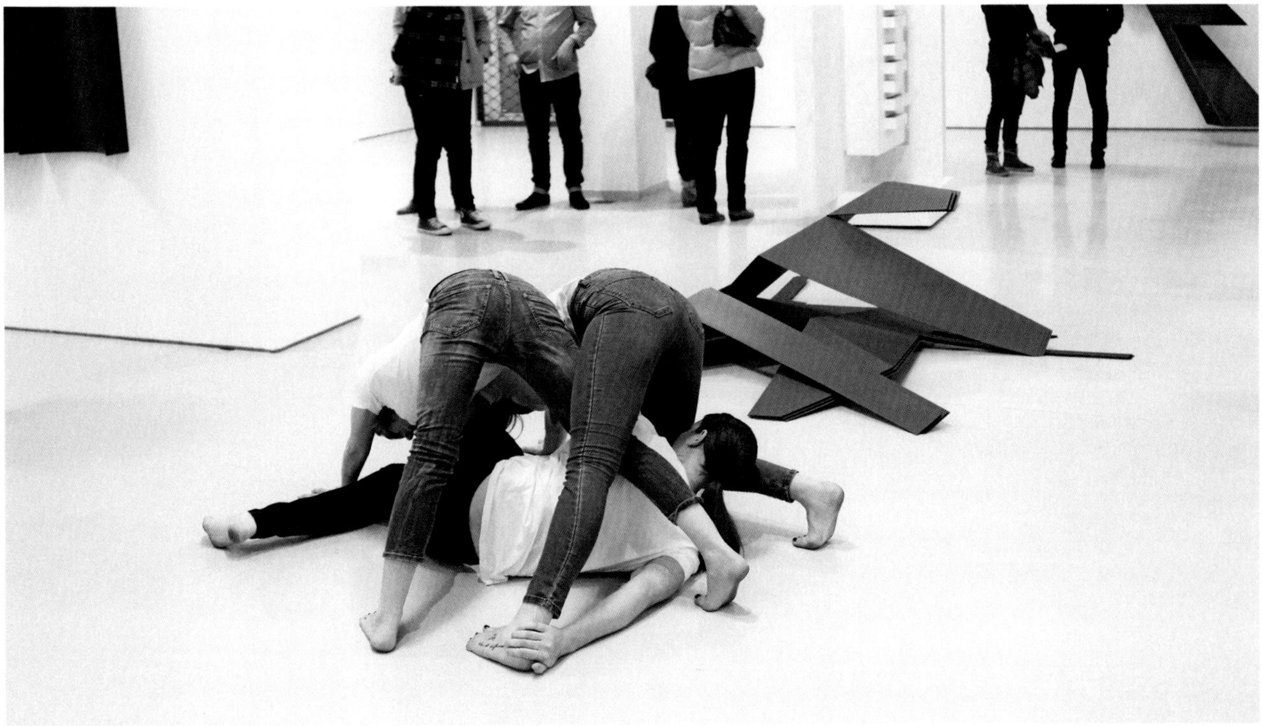

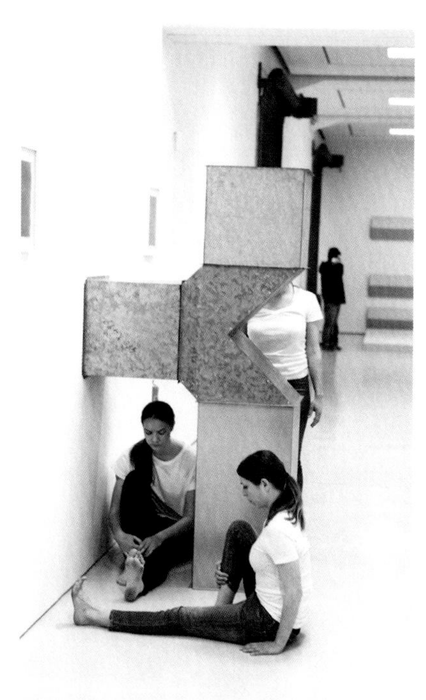

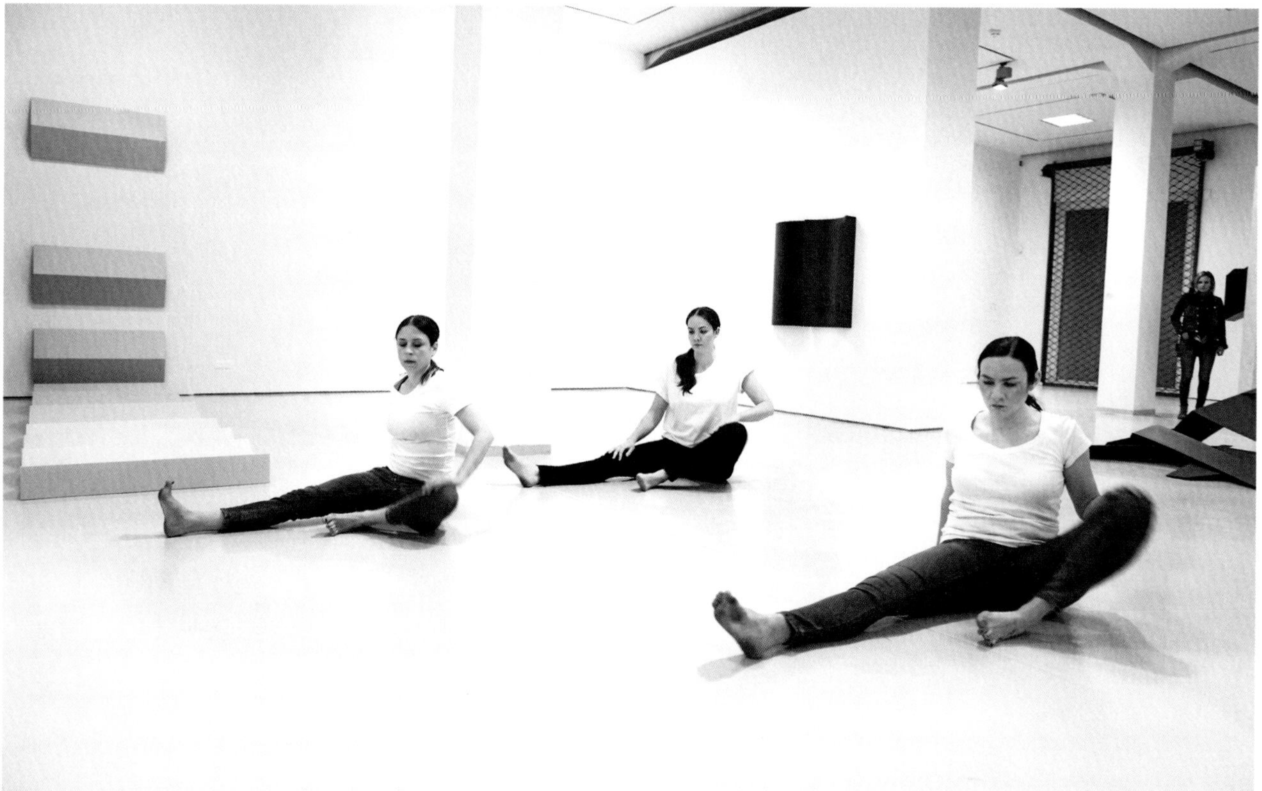

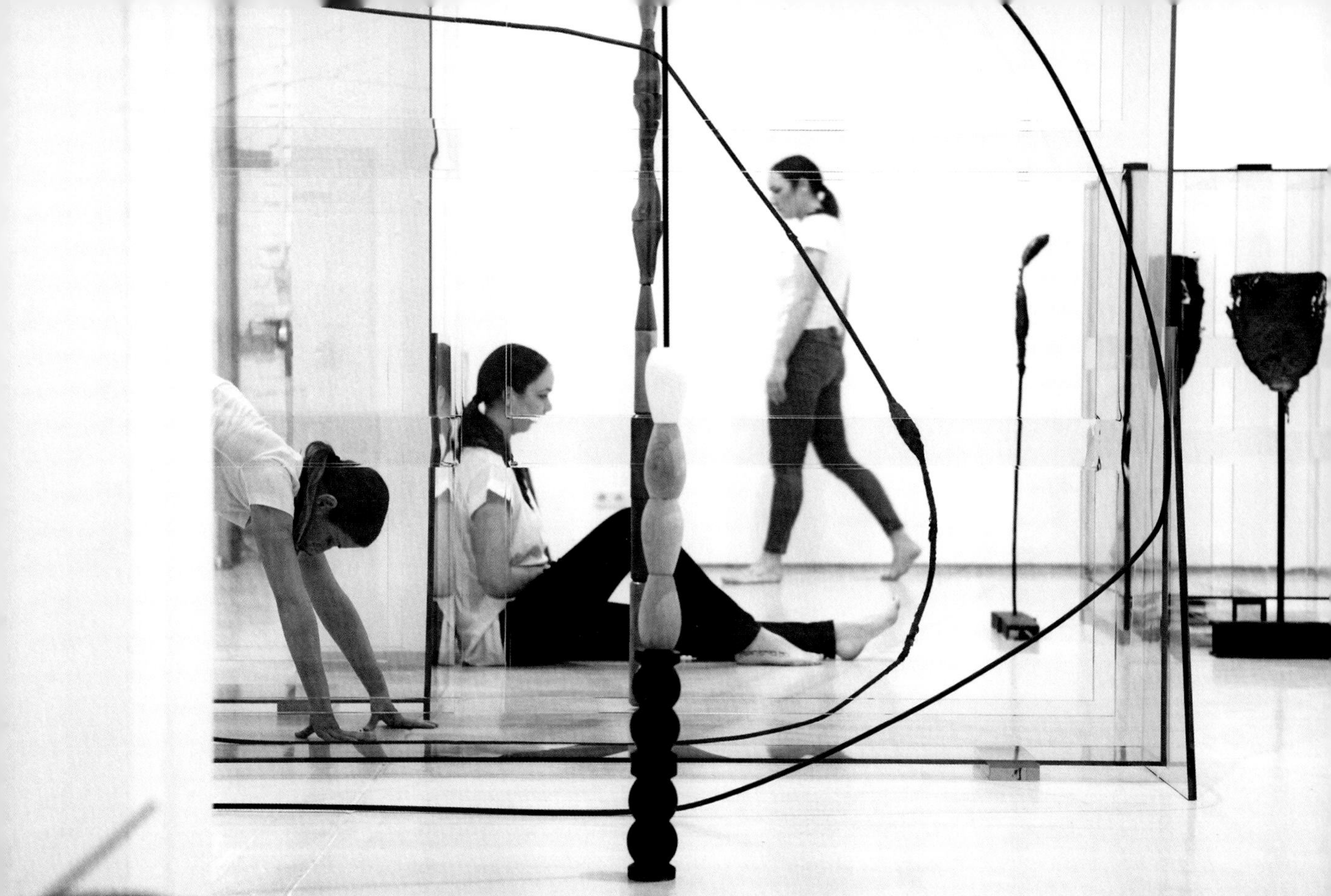

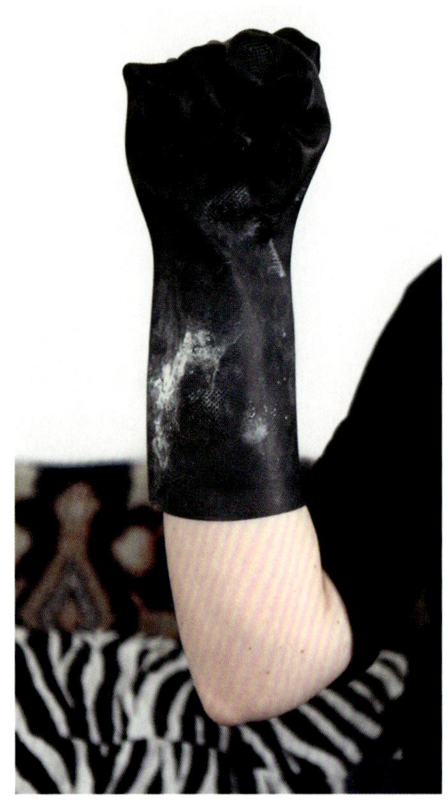
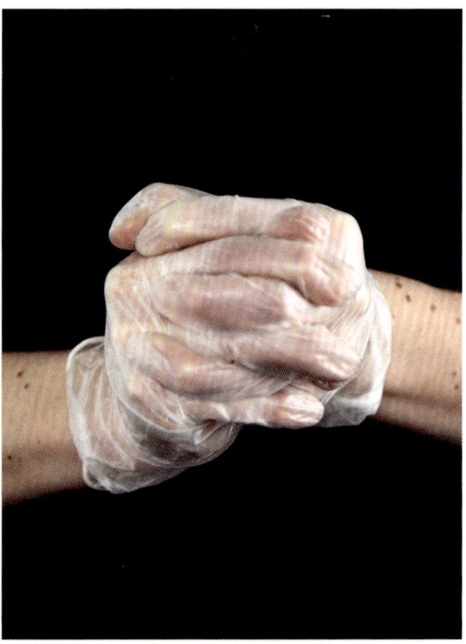
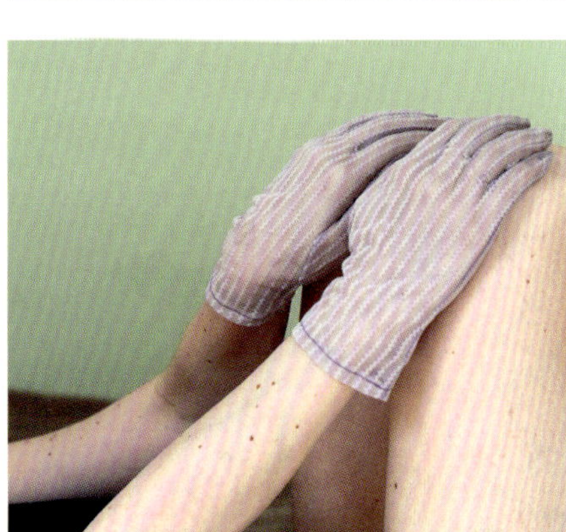
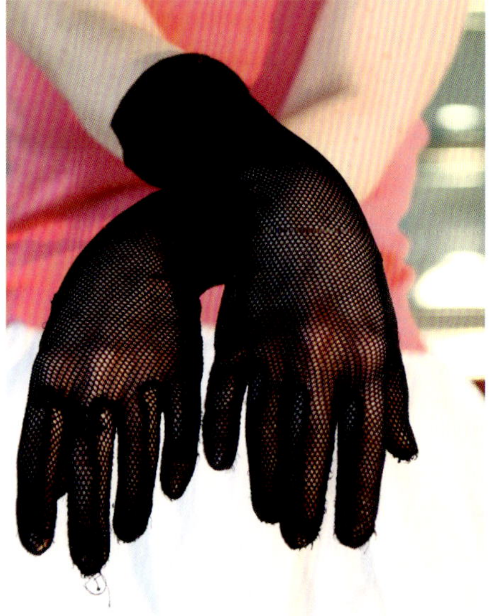

GLOVES, 2012
detail

ZWISCHEN INNENSEITE UND AUSSENSEITE KONFUSION ERZEUGEN[1]

Doris Krystof

Hals aus Gummi

Maren Maurer hat vom Tanz kommend einen bildkünstlerischen Ansatz mit einer großen Bandbreite entwickelt. So unterschiedlich ihre Skulpturen, Zeichnungen, Aquarelle, Fotografien, Installationen, Performances und Videoprojektionen auch erscheinen mögen, immer stellt der Raum eine feste Bezugsgröße ihrer Arbeiten dar. Raum meint dabei ebenso bekanntes Terrain wie noch unerschlossene Regionen. „Hic sunt dracones" (hier sind Drachen) lautet die auf mittelalterlichen Landkarten gebräuchliche Formel zur Kennzeichnung unwägbarer Gebiete, eine Formel, die durch ihre Verwendung im Kontext des Chaos Computer Clubs den Sprung in die Gegenwart geschafft hat und auch Maurers erstem Werkkatalog einen treffenden Titel zu liefern vermag. Offene, undefinierte, prekäre Stellen spielen nämlich in Maurers Werk eine konstitutive Rolle. Das zeigt sich in ihren stets sorgfältig arrangierten Ausstellungen, in denen Leere in Gestalt der Abstände zwischen den Exponaten eine genauso wichtige Rolle spielt wie das Weiß des Papiers in ihren Aquarellen und Zeichnungen mit den leichten, oftmals wie hingehaucht wirkenden Motiven. Der leere Raum als suggestive, vom Theater als offenes Experimentierfeld gedeutete Größe (Peter Brook 1968) wirkt bei der Bildhauerin indes auch in einem durchaus traditionell plastischen und konkreten Sinne nach. Seit 2012/2013 entstehen vermehrt im klassischen Abgussverfahren erzeugte Formen, die mit dem Wechsel von Positiv- und Negativform experimentieren und Raum als eine Form des Dazwischen charakterisieren. Unterschiedlichste Materialien wie Aluminium, Kunststoff, Gummi und in jüngster Zeit sogar das altehrwürdige Material Bronze kommen zum Einsatz – und immer wieder auch der Körper der Künstlerin beziehungsweise ein Teil davon. Ein Beispiel ist die aus zwei Ballons zusammengefügte, noch unbetitelte Skulptur, die durch ein seltsam geformtes Verbindungselement zusammengehalten wird „Gewisser Aufstand" [Seite 17]. Dabei handelt es sich um einen aus Gummi gefertigten Abguss des Halses der Künstlerin, was der Skulptur Fragilität, ja geradezu den Eindruck von existenzieller Gefährdung verleiht. Der überraschend aus dem körperlichen Zusammenhang herausgelöste und freigestellte Hals ist als solcher kaum wiederzuerkennen. Wo war schon je ein Hals ohne Kopf ganz für sich alleine zu sehen? Oder ein Hals mit zwei Köpfen? Maurer mischt narrativ inhaltliche Aspekte mit abstrakten Formen und überführt die Physis der Objekte in eine psychische Dimension, die virtuos zwischen den Parametern Raum, Körper und Material aufgespannt ist.

Raum, Körper, Material

Maren Maurer schloss an ihre Ausbildung und Praxis in klassischem Bühnentanz ein Studium an der Düsseldorfer Kunstakademie bei Rita McBride und Rosemarie Trockel an. Nach der Akademie führte sie ein Stipendium nach Tel Aviv, wo sie nicht nur bildkünstlerisch arbeitete, sondern am Suzanne Delall Center auch die Gaga-Tanzklassen von Ohad Naharin besuchte. Als Reaktion auf die Erfahrung des äußerst vitalen, in der Gruppe praktizierten Tanzes entstand die Reihe der „Nanas" – 20 Zeichnungen von Händen in unterschiedlichen Haltungen, die teils mit Objekten wie Würfeln oder Schnüren kombiniert sind [Seite 71–77]. Maurer verarbeitete in den Assemblagen nicht nur die dem Gaga-Tanz zugrunde liegende starke Bedeutung der aus der Körpermitte heraus entwickelten Handhaltungen. Mit der zeichnerischen Deklination der Gebärden reagierte Maurer auch auf die Erfahrung, inwiefern in einem Land mit einer ihr unbekannten Sprache Kommunikation über den Ausdruck des Körpers und vor allem der Hände funktioniert. Das Motiv der Hand verfolgte Maurer nach ihrer Rückkehr aus Israel intensiv weiter. In der Ausstellung „Changing Conditions", 2012 in der Düsseldorfer Galerie COSAR HMT, verarbeitete sie das Thema Hand in unterschiedlichster Gestalt und Materialität zu einem kohärenten Konzept. Wieder spielte der leere Raum, ein 240 m^2 großer Saal im ehemals von Nonnen bewohnten Haus Maria Theresia, eine zentrale Rolle bei der Präsentation und Wahrnehmung der sparsam gesetzten Arbeiten. Zwischen zwei freistehenden Säulen war über eine Strecke von ca. fünf Metern ein dünnes Kupferband aufgehängt, das an beiden Seiten an zwei spiegelverkehrt einander gegenüber an der Wand montierten Händen befestigt war [Seite 4–6]. Sorgfältig halten die beiden verkupferten Bronzehände jeweils ein Ende des schmalen und leicht durchhängenden sowie einmal gedrehten Bandes zwischen Daumen und Mittelfinger. Mit der zeremoniellen Gebärde erinnert die skulpturale Installation „ich , was" (2011) an den in asiatischen Kulturen gepflegten Brauch, eine Ausstellung durch das Zerschneiden eines Bandes zu eröffnen. Neben dem die Horizontale akzentuierenden Band gab es in der Ausstellung eine zweite vertikal frei im Raum hängende Skulptur, eine an der Decke befestigte und fast bis zum Boden reichende Kette aus neun miteinander verbundenen Händepaaren [Seite 59–61]. Obwohl sie von der Decke hing, schien sich die Kette gegen alle Gesetze der Schwerkraft in einer serpentinenförmigen Bewegung von unten nach oben zu schrauben. Maurers Bronze-Arbeit „as helpful as adjustable" (2012), in der die ringförmig aufeinander gelegten Fingerspitzen von Daumen und Zeigefinger die einzelnen Kettenglieder bilden, erzeugt durch die serielle Reihung von gleichen Modulen eine potenziell unendliche Komposition. Zur Ausstellung gehörten schließlich auch „Gloves" [Seite 64–69] – drei fotografische Tableaus, die das Thema Hand in einem anderen Medium vorführen. Auf jeweils einem an der Wand befestigten schmalen Regalbrett sind vier (einmal auch fünf) Fotografien unterschiedlichen Formats von Maurers Händen in unterschiedlichsten Handschuhen arrangiert. Bilder mit eleganten langen Satinhandschuhen, groben Gummihandschuhen, feinsten Spitzenprodukten und einfachen Wollhandschuhen stehen wie in einer Auslage nebeneinander. In dem eindringlichen Spektrum weiblicher Händepaare wechseln sich graziöse Posen mit manierierten oder sogar verkrampften Haltungen ab, wobei erstere an Hollywoodglamour und letztere an die aus dem Umkreis von Charcot und Freud bekannten Illustrationen weiblicher Hysterie um 1900 erinnern. Die Kombination aus Bronze und Fotografie in dieser Ausstellung erzeugte einen spannungsvollen Gegensatz, wobei sich die Fotos im hinteren Teil der Ausstellung wie zeitgenössische visuelle Referenzen zu den ehernen Bronzehänden im vorderen Bereich ausnahmen. Ein Mix unterschiedlicher Materialien zeigt sich schließlich in einer Arbeit wie „Changing Conditions" (2012) [Seite 62–63]. Wieder scheinen zwei Hände aus der Wand zu wachsen, dieses Mal haben sie zwischen gespreiztem Daumen und kleinem Finger ein elastisches Band aufgespannt. Die parallel über eine Strecke von 149 cm (exakt die Spannweite der Künstlerin) in geringem Abstand vor der Wand geführten Linien beschreiben eine Diagonale – und damit eine Form, die auch eine andere, zunächst vollständig abstrakt wirkende plastische Arbeit bestimmt. Bei der rot patinierten Bronze „Diagonal (David)" (2014) [Seite 18, 19] handelt es sich um den diagonalen Ausschnitt eines männlichen Torsos von der rechten Hüfte bis zur linken Schulter. Die rätselhafte Form der „Körper-Scheibe" beschreibt eine scheinbar aus der Achse gekippte Stele und verdankt sich wiederum einer Anregung aus der Bewegungslehre. In der Körperarbeit des israelischen Ingenieurs und Körpertherapeuten Moshé Feldenkrais („Bewusstheit durch Bewegung", 1968) spielt das Erspüren der Diagonale eine wichtige Rolle. Etwas so ephemeres wie das Bewusstwerden einer körperlichen Erfahrung ist in eine kompakte plastische Form übertragen.

Die Hand der Künstlerin

Die räumlich-körperliche Dimension von Skulptur, ihr leiblich physischer Aspekt, schließt bei Maurer vielfach an eigene Bewegungserfahrungen an, die eine besondere Form der Wahrnehmung darstellen. Auch in ihren Performances, wie der am 18. April 2015 in der Ausstellung „Broken Spaces" im Düsseldorfer Ausstellungsraum Kai 10 mit zwei weiteren Akteurinnen (Lavinia und Sirkka Muth) aufgeführten dreistündigen Liveperformance „CHAKRAPENG!", geht es um Wahrnehmung, körperliches Erleben, um ein sinnliches Nachempfinden der ausgestellten Skulpturen von Charlotte Posenenske, Benjamin Houlihan, Tatiana Trouvé u. a. [Seite 41–45]. Körper, Auge und Hand vermitteln Welterkenntnis. Im Motiv der Hand fallen Greifen und Begreifen zusammen; Tasten, Fühlen und Zeigen sind, wie jedes Kind weiß, zentrale Kategorien von Wissenserwerb. Maurers „Hand-Arbeiten" stehen zudem emblematisch für die bildhauerische Tätigkeit, die im Abdruck der Hand in formbarem Material ihren Ursprung hat. Vielfältige per Hand ausgeführte plastische Tätigkeiten wie Kneten, Formen, Streichen oder

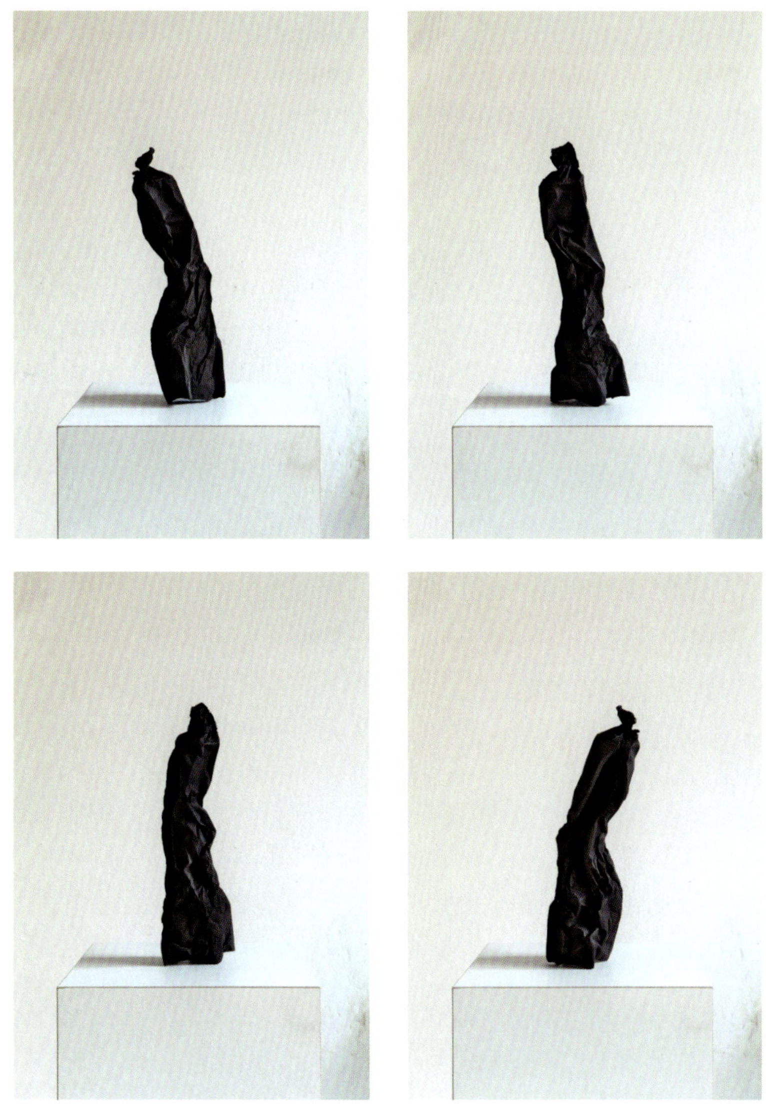

CRUMPLE (ROCKET), 2014
patinized bronze on pedestal
44 x 8 x 8,7 cm

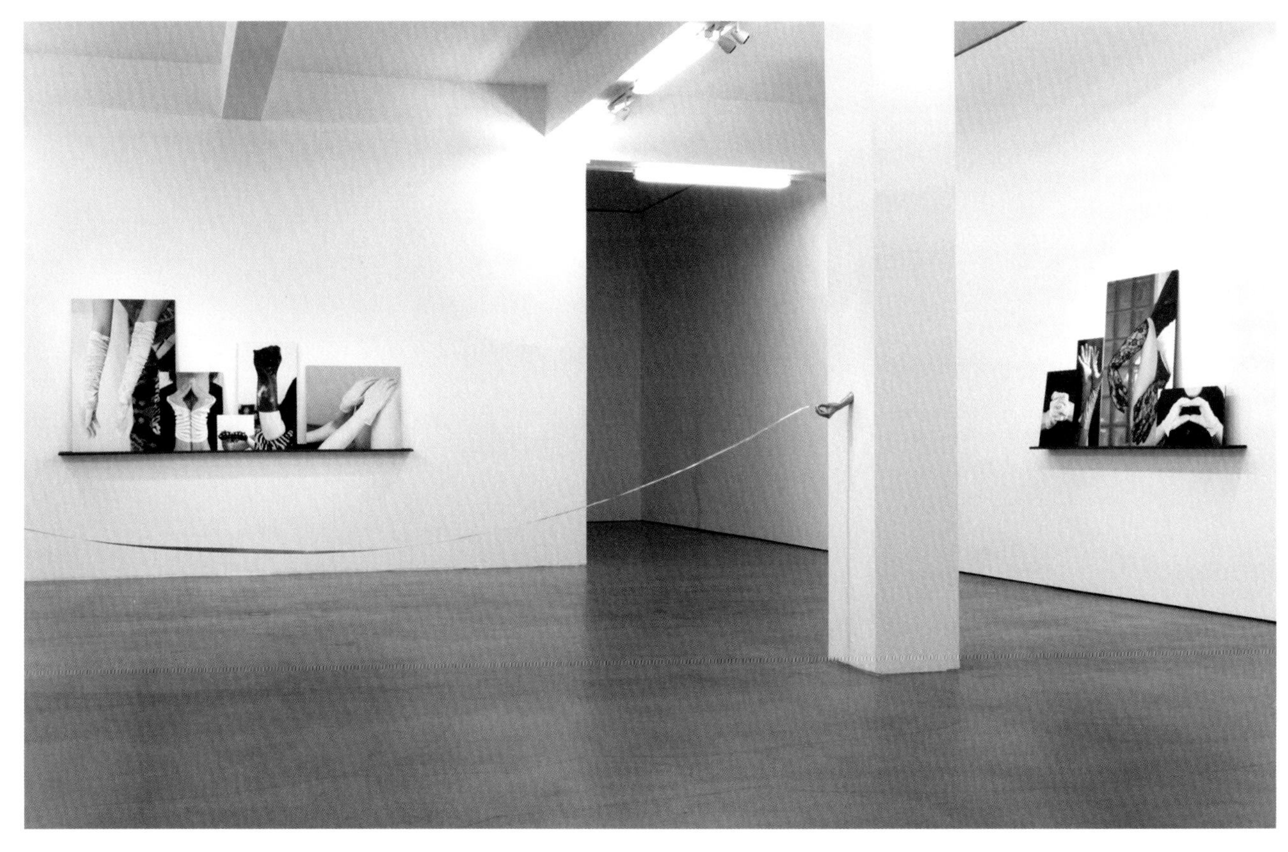

CHANGING CONDITIONS
11.05.2012, COSAR HMT

Falten finden sich in Maurers Arbeiten in den Skulpturen selbst thematisiert. Hier ist zum Beispiel die seit 2013 entstehende Werkgruppe der „Crumples", Metallgüsse von zusammengedrücktem Papier, die mit oder ohne Patinierung unterschiedliche Oberflächenwirkungen erzeugen [Seite 24, 32–35, 36–37, 38, 39], zu nennen. In der Ausstellung „Breathe Normally" (2014) wirkten die „Crumples" aus Bronze, die in dem kleinen Ausstellungsraum in Düsseldorf-Oberkassel zu der Installation „wir teilen" arrangiert waren, wie semitransparentes, wächsernes Backpapier, zerknüllt und achtlos auf den Boden geworfen. Daneben der illustre an der Wand installierte Aluminiumguss „Mirror, Mirror" (2014) [Seite 14–15], der mit seinen seriellen Quadraten auf ein gefaltetes Blatt Papier zurückgeht. Maurer entwickelt mit den unterschiedlichen Abgusstechniken ein um Begriffe wie Nachahmung, Mimesis, Imitation, Kopie und Fake kreisendes Formrepertoire. Ein per Post ins Atelier gelangtes Verpackungsmaterial stellt sich in Bronze gegossen als erlesenes Relief mit informellen Ahnen dar [Seite 79]. Die Bronzeskulptur „Annabelle" (2013) hingegen eliminiert die Verpackung, zeigt Kartoffeln wie aufgehäuft in einem Sack und lässt die formgebende Hülle einfach weg [Seite 09]. Wie eine gigantische minimale Plastik nimmt sich der Abguss einer Rolle zur Abdichtung von Fenstern oder Türen aus [Seite 88]. Und die überkreuz gelegten Baumstöcke „Raute (Brandenburg)" [Seite 90–91] verraten nur bei genauem Hinsehen, dass es sich auch hier um Bronze handelt, die die Formen der Natur in ein alle Zeiten überdauerndes ewiges Material übersetzt. Dass dies explizit ganz ohne Pathos geschieht, spricht für eine Künstlergeneration, die aufbauend auf Positionen von Thomas Schütte oder Rosemarie Trockel, das Handwerkliche und den Rückgriff auf tradierte Materialien mit konzeptioneller Leichtigkeit erneut erprobt.

Die Hand des Künstlers steht am Anfang der Kunstgeschichte, als mit dem programmatischen Begriff „maniera", in dem nicht zufällig das lateinische Wort für Hand („manus") steckt, für eine Emanzipation des bildenden Künstlers von der als bloßes Handwerk verstandenen, in Zünften organisierten bildenden Kunst gekämpft wurde. Unter dem Motto „ut pictura poesis" (dass Malerei wie ein Gedicht sei) wurde im 16. Jahrhundert erst in Italien und dann in den Niederlanden für eine Kunst gestritten, die Theorie und Praxis, Hand und Kopf, Poesie und bildende Kunst zusammenbrachte. Damit war die Basis für die Ausbildung des neuzeitlichen Künstlersubjekts gelegt, was in zahlreichen Darstellungen von Künstlerhänden von Raffael über Rubens bis hin zu Bruce Nauman zum Ausdruck kommt. Wenn heute eine Künstlerin diese Tradition künstlerischer Selbstreflexion streift, ist damit ein weiteres Statement abgegeben, auch wenn sich im Fall von Maren Maurer die Artikulation eines weiblichen künstlerischen Selbstverständnisses mit der Disziplin tänzerischer Übung und den darin erprobten Haltungen (auch der Hände) überlagert. Schließlich hat sich in Maurers Ansatz ein weiterer Aspekt aus der Zeit des Manierismus in das frühe 21. Jahrhundert herübergerettet. Wurde doch am Beginn der frühen Neuzeit eine Kunstlehre ausgebildet, die im Wissen um den produktiven Widerspruch von Sein und Schein, innerem Kern und äußerer Schale gründet. In Maurers Werk findet man etliche Beispiele solch einer Als-ob-Ästhetik, so die bereits erwähnten bronzenen Äste, aber auch eine in Aluminium gegossene Kapsel, wie sie zur Zubereitung von Espresso verwendet wird [Seite 55]. Oder die kleine rote aus Gips geformte Skulptur mit dem Titel „Roma", die Maurer in der Gemüsetheke des Supermarkts ausgewogen und mit einem Klebeetikett versehen hat [Seite 54]. Als ob der Preis einer echten Tomate identisch mit dem einer Kleinplastik wäre, verkehrt sich das Verhältnis von äußerer Schale und innerem Wert. Die in der Bildhauerei seit jeher immer wieder aufs Neue befragte Relation von Innen und Außen nimmt Maurer dankend auf. Als Verwirrspiel treibt sie das Konzept der verlorenen Form weiter, trägt eine Gipstomate in den Supermarkt, zieht einen Sack Kartoffeln ohne Sack hervor und steckt ihre Hände in die Negativform von Handschuhen – ganz so als wolle sie in ihren plastischen Arbeiten, um es mit Bruce Nauman zu sagen, „zwischen der Innenseite und der Außenseite einer Arbeit Konfusion erzeugen (...)".

[1] *Bruce Nauman in: Interview with Willoughby Sharp (1970), hier zitiert nach: Janet Kraynak (ed.), Please pay attention: Bruce Nauman' s words. Writings and interviews. The MIT Press, Cambridge/Massachusetts, London/England 2003, S. 117.*

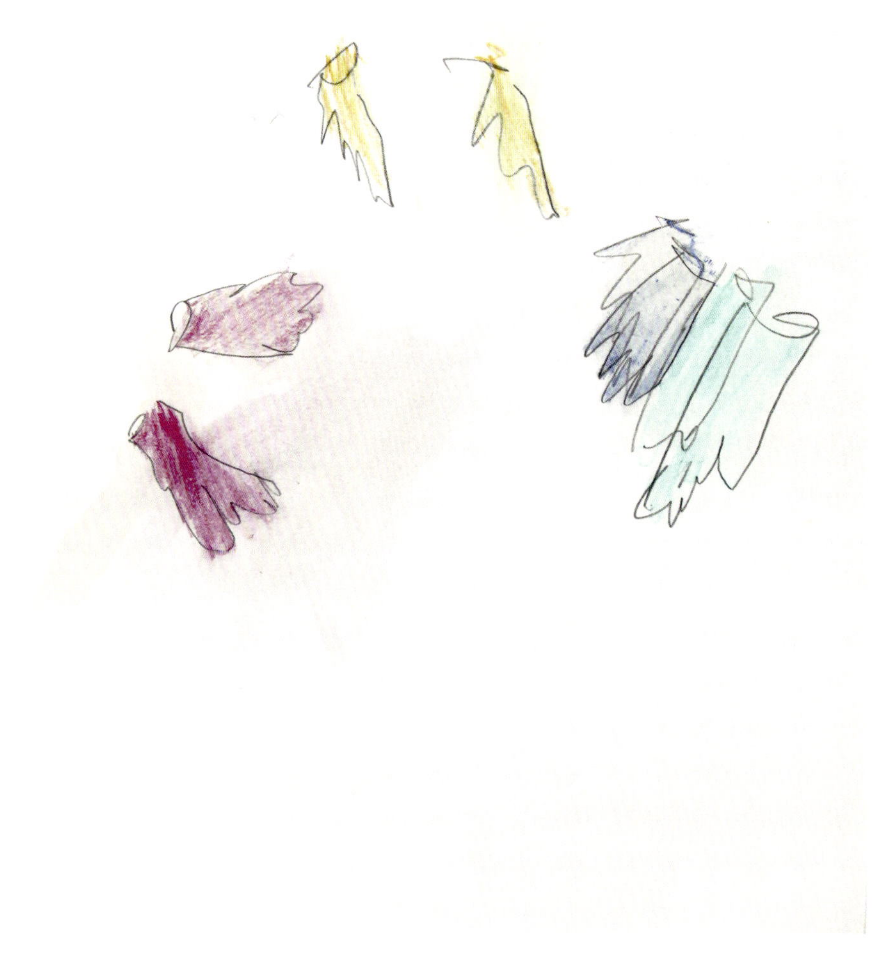

ONE ANOTHER, 2012
pencil, watercolor
31 x 21 cm

CREATING CONFUSION BETWEEN INSIDE AND OUTSIDE[1]

Doris Krystof

A neck made of rubber

Maren Maurer developed her broad visual-artistic approach on the basis of her training as a dancer. Her sculptures, drawings, watercolors, photographs, installations, performances and video projections may seem very diverse, yet there is a reference value that plays a part in all of her works, and that is space. Here space is taken to mean both familiar terrain or unexplored regions. "Hic sunt dracones" (here be dragons) is the formula used to designate unchartable areas on medieval maps – a formula that has found its way into today's popular culture through its use by the Chaos Computer Club, and which provides a fitting title for Maurer's first catalog of works. Indeed, open, undefined and precarious sections play a constitutive role in Maurer's oeuvre. This can be seen in her exhibitions, which she always carefully curates. Absence, in the guise of the distance between the exhibits, plays an important role here. This type of space is as important to her work as the white of the paper in her watercolors and drawings, in which the light motifs often seem as though they have been breathed onto the page. Empty space as a suggestive value and which is interpreted in theater as an open field of experimentation (Peter Brook, 1968) continues to have an effect in the artist's work in a quite traditional sculptural and concrete sense. Since 2012/2013, she has increasingly been using classic casting processes to create structures that play with the shift between positive and negative shapes and which characterize space as a kind of in-betweenness. Maurer uses diverse materials, such as aluminum, plastic, rubber and, most recently, even the revered material bronze. Time and again, the artist's body will also become part of her work. One example of this is a sculpture, "Gewisser Aufstand", made up of two balloons that have been joined together by an oddly shaped connecting element [page 17]. The connecting part is a rubber cast of the artist's neck. This lends the sculpture a sense of fragility, even some kind of existential danger. The cropped neck is almost unrecognizable as such and is a surprising sight in its separation from the rest of the body. Where do we ever encounter a neck without the corresponding head it holds purely on its own? Or a neck with two heads? Maurer interweaves narrative elements and abstract shapes, translating the physical body of the objects into a psychological dimension that is virtuously unfurled between the parameters of space, body and material.

Space, body, material

After training and working as a classical concert dancer, Maren Maurer studied at Kunstakademie Düsseldorf under Rita McBride and Rosemarie Trockel. After completing her studies, a scholarship brought her to Tel Aviv, where she both worked artistically and attended Ohad Naharin's Gaga dance classes at the Suzanne Delall Center. As a response to her experience of the extremely lively dance form practiced in the group Maurer produced the "Nanas" series – 20 drawings of hands in different poses are combined with objects such as dice or pieces of string – [pages 71–77].

It was not just the strong meaning of the hand positions developed out of the body core underlying Gaga dance that Maurer addressed in her assemblages.

For Maurer's graphic declination of these gestures is also a reaction to the experience of how one communicates with one's hands and body in a country in which one does not know the native language. She continued to engage with the motif of the hand even after returning from Israel. In the exhibition "Changing Conditions," held at Düsseldorf gallery COSAR HMT in 2012, she explored the hand motif in all kinds of forms and materials, establishing a coherent concept. Empty space, in this case a hall of 240 square meters in Maria Theresia House, a former nunnery, played a central role once more in the presentation and perception of the sparingly placed works. A thin copper band spanning about five meters was hung between two freestanding columns. This was held by two hands, one on each side, mounted on the wall to mirror each other [pages 4–6]. The two copper-coated bronze hands carefully gripped one end of the strip each between thumb and middle finger. The strip sagged slightly and had been twisted once. The ceremonial gesture referenced in the sculptural installation "ich , was" (2011) could be read as being reminiscent of the opening of an exhibition by cutting a ribbon, as practiced in Asian cultures. Along with the wire accentuating the horizontal, Maurer also exhibited a second, vertical sculpture freely suspended in the space. A chain of nine pairs of hands, connected to each other and dangling from the ceiling almost all the way down to the floor [pages 59–61]. Despite hanging from the ceiling, the chain seemed to defy gravity and spiral upward in a serpentine movement. Maurer's bronze piece "as helpful as adjustable" (2012), in which the rings formed by the touching fingertips of thumb and index fingers make up the individual chain links, creates a potentially endless composition. The identical modules can be strung together serially. Finally, the exhibition also featured "Gloves" (pages 64–69), three photographic tableaus that elaborate the hand theme in a different medium. Thin shelves affixed to the wall each hold a careful arrangement of four (with one holding five) differently sized photographs of Maurer's hands in very different kinds of gloves. Pictures with elegant long satin gloves, crude rubber versions, the most delicate of lace handwear and simple woolen mitts are placed next to one another as if on display. In the vivid spectrum of female pairs of hands, graceful poses alternate with affected and even tense gestures – with the former calling to mind Hollywood glamor and the latter illustrations of female hysteria as would have been made in Freudian or Charcotian circles around 1900. The combination of bronze and photography created an exciting juxtaposition in the exhibition, with the photos in the rear part of the show appearing to be contemporary visual references to the sturdy bronze hands in the front section. Finally, Maurer uses a mixture of dif-

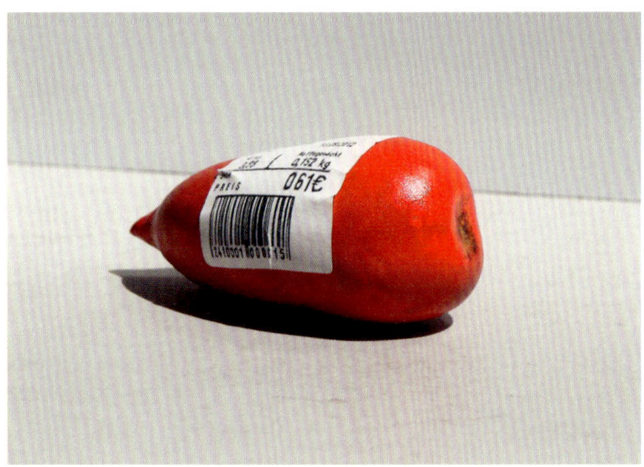

ROMA, 2012
plaster, color, pencil on paper
9 x 5 x 4,3 cm

ferent materials in the piece "Changing Conditions" (2012) [pages 62–63)]. Here, two hands once again seem to grow out of the wall, but this time an elastic string is stretched between their splayed thumbs and little fingers. The parallel lines created by the rubber band close to the wall span a distance of 149 cm, which is the exact span of the artist's arms. They form a diagonal, a shape that also defines another three-dimensional piece that seems entirely abstract at first glance. The bronze "Diagonal (David)" (2014) [pages 18, 19], with its red patina, is a cast of a diagonal section of a male torso from the right hip to the left shoulder. The enigmatic shape of this "slice of body" can best be described as resembling a stele that seemingly has been tilted off-axis and is again inspired by kinematics. Sensing the diagonal plays an important part in the body work of Israeli engineer and body therapist Moshé Feldenkrais ("Awareness Through Movement", 1968). Maurer translates into a compact three-dimensional shape something that is as ephemeral as becoming aware of a physical experience.

The artist's hand

The spatio-physical dimension of sculpture, its bodily aspect, connects to Maurer's own experiences of physical movement, which constitute a special type of perception. Her performances, such as the three-hour live performance "CHAKRAPENG!," which she held on April 18, 2015 in the "Broken Spaces" exhibition in the Düsseldorf exhibition space Kai 10 together with two other performers (Lavinia and Sirkka Muth), are also about perception, physical experience and a sensory understanding of the sculptures exhibited by Charlotte Posenenske, Benjamin Houlihan, Tatiana Trouvé and others [pages 41–45]. Body, eye and hand convey knowledge of the world. The theme of the hand visualizes grasping, both in a physical and an intellectual sense. As every child knows, touching, feeling and showing are key ways of acquiring knowledge. Maurer's "hand pieces" are also emblematic of sculptural work based on the im-

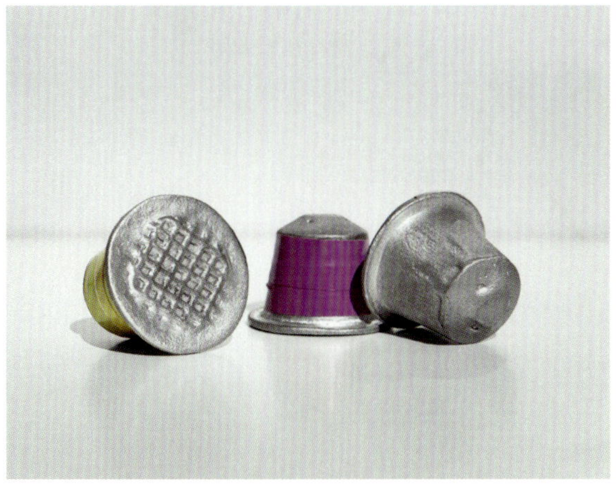

CUPS (KAMPF UND KÖPFE), 2013
aluminium, tape
each 3 x Ø 3,7 cm

pression left by a hand in malleable material. Many activities carried out by hand, such as kneading, shaping, stroking or folding, are actually addressed in and by Maurer's sculptures. An example of this is the work group "Crumples," produced since 2013. It consists of metal casts of scrunched-up pieces of paper that create different surface effects with or without patination [pages 24, 32–35, 36–37, 38, 39]. In the exhibition "Breathe Normally" (2014), the bronze "Crumples" – arranged to form the installation "wir teilen" in the small exhibition space in Düsseldorf's Oberkassel district – resembled semi-transparent waxed baking paper, crumpled up and carelessly tossed aside. With its serial squares, the shiny aluminum cast "Mirror, Mirror" (2014) [pages 14–15] installed on the wall next to "Crumples" is based on a folded piece of paper. With the different casting techniques Maurer develops a repertoire of shapes that revolves around notions such as imitation, mimesis, copy and fake. Packaging material reaching her studio by post morphs into a delicate relief rooted in abstract art when cast in bronze [page 79]. By contrast, the bronze sculpture "Annabelle" (2013) eliminates packaging. It shows potatoes in a pile as though held together by a sack, but the bag the defines the shape does not feature [page 09]. A cast made from a reel of insulating sealant for windows and doors looks like an enormous minimal sculpture [page 88]. And the tree trunks placed across each other in "Raute (Brandenburg)" [pages 90, 91] only reveal that they are made of bronze on closer inspection, with the natural shapes translated into an imperishable material. The fact that this is done without any pathos whatsoever speaks in favor of a generation of artists who with great conceptual lightness and drawing on the artistic positions of Thomas Schütte or Rosemarie Trockel, are again trying out both traditional materials and hand craftsmanship.

The artist's hand marks the beginning of art history, when fine artists fought for vocational freedom from being the crafts guilds and for emancipation from a role as mere craftsmen - taking as their programmatic slogan the term term "maniera," which by no coincidence derives from the Latin word for hand ("manus"). In the 16th century artists in Italy and, later on, in the Netherlands fought for an art that combined theory and practice, hand and head, poetry and visual art under the motto "ut pictura poesis" (as is painting so is poetry). This laid the foundations for the development of the modern individual artist, as expressed in countless depictions of artists' hands from Raphael

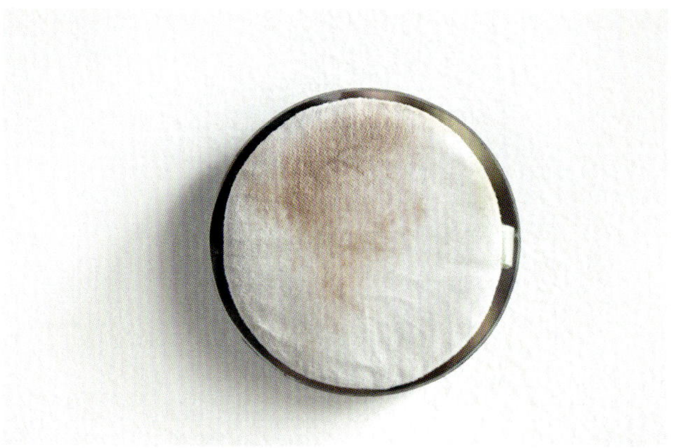

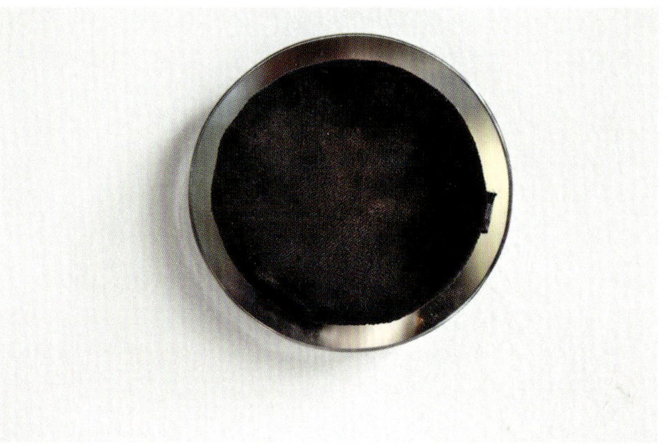

KOMPROMISS UND BEZIEHUNG, 2012
mirror, powder puff
1,5 x Ø 12 cm

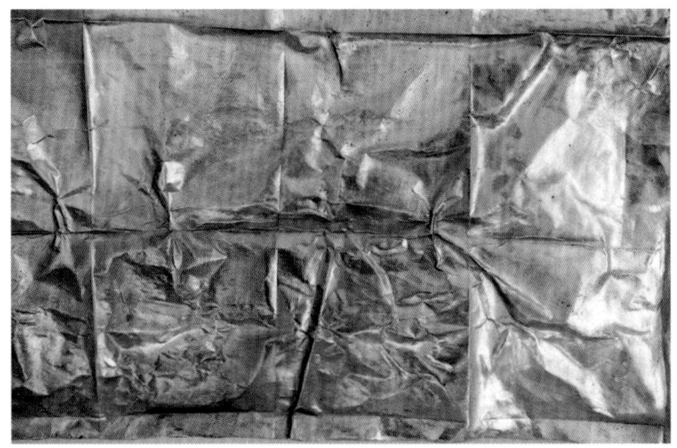

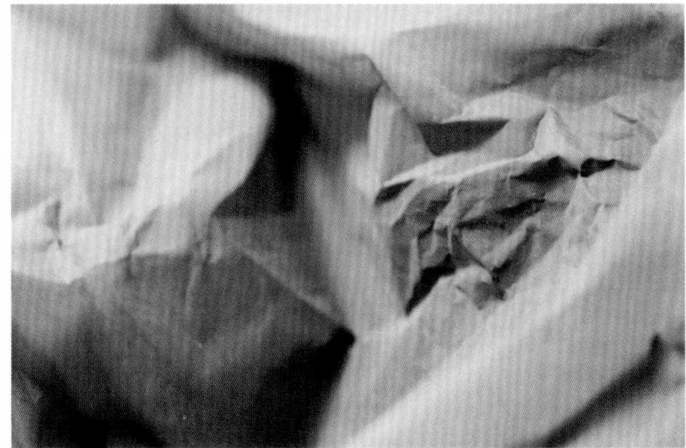

detail **MIRROR, MIRROR**
detail **CRUMPLE (OMA)**

to Rubens to Bruce Nauman. If a female artist touches upon this tradition of artistic self-reflection today, we can read this as a further statement, even if in the case of Maren Maurer's work the articulation of a female artistic self-conception is superimposed onto the discipline of dance practice and the poses (of the body, including the hands) assumed as part of this. Ultimately a further Mannerist-era aspect has through Maurer's artistic approach been salvaged for the early 21st century. In the early modern period a theory of art was formed based on the knowledge of the productive contradiction between existence and semblance, inner core and outer shell. Maurer's oeuvre contains numerous examples of this kind of as-if aesthetic, for example the previously mentioned bronze branches, as well as an aluminum-cast capsule, such as those used to make espresso [page 55]. There is also the small red sculpture made of plaster entitled "Roma", which Maurer weighed using the vegetable scales in a supermarket, and placing the label onto the object [page 54]. As though the price of a real tomato were identical to that of a small sculpture, the relationship between outer shell and core value is reversed. Maurer gratefully responds to the question as to the relationship between inside and outside, a question sculptors have been asking since time immemorial. She advances the concept of the lost form or mold in a game of deliberate confusion by taking a plaster tomato to the supermarket, producing a sack of potatoes without the sack and putting her hands in the negative form of gloves. To use the words of Bruce Nauman, it seems as though in her sculptural works she is intent on "creating confusion between the inside and the outside of a work (...)."

[1] *Bruce Nauman in: Interview with Willoughby Sharp (1970), cited: Janet Kraynak (ed.), Please pay attention: Bruce Nauman's words. Writings and interviews. The MIT Press, Cambridge/Massachusetts, London/England 2003, p. 117.*

S. / pp. 59–61

AS HELPFUL AS ADJUSTABLE, 2012
patinized bronze
380 x Ø 16 cm
Installation COSAR HMT

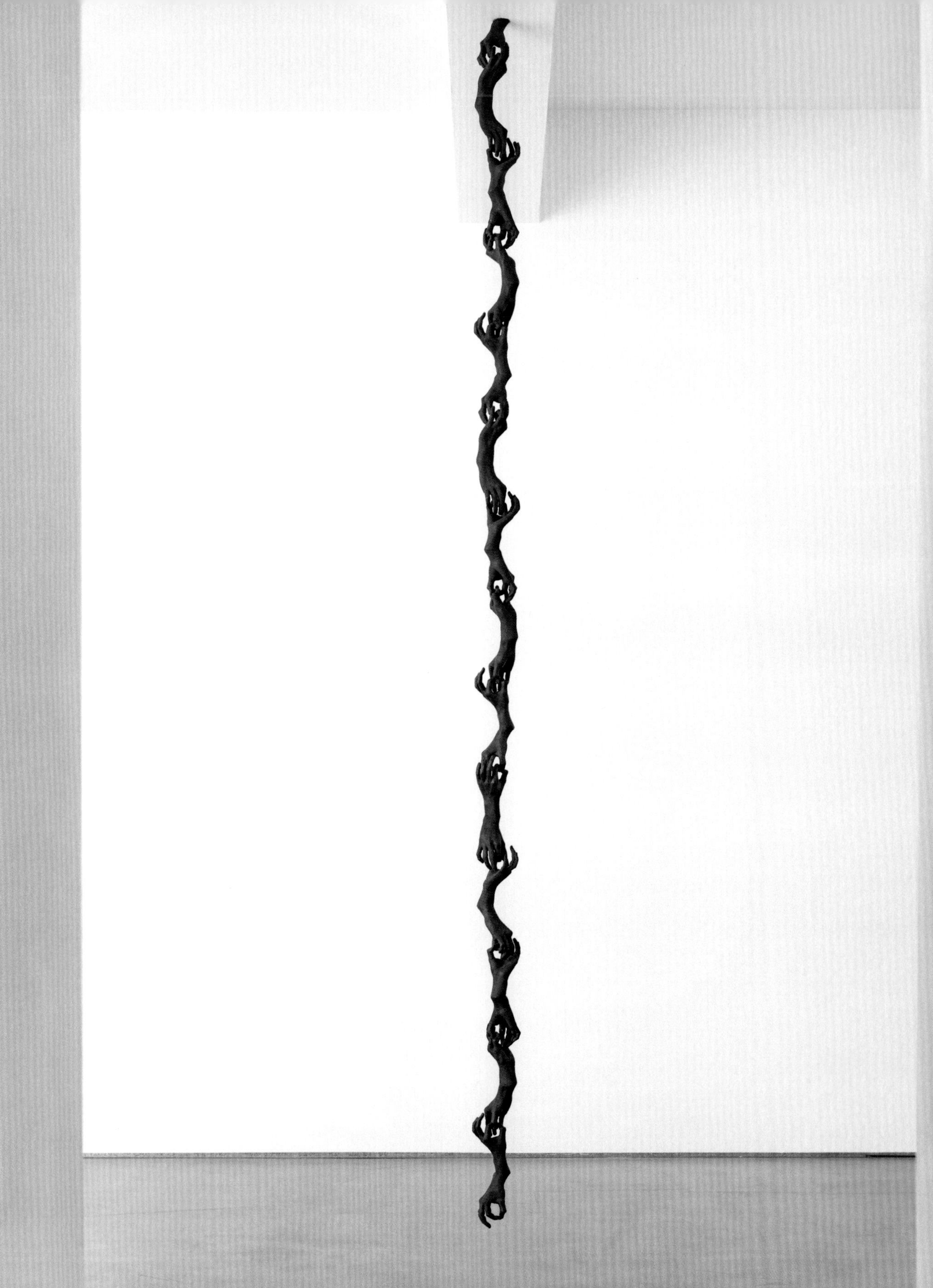

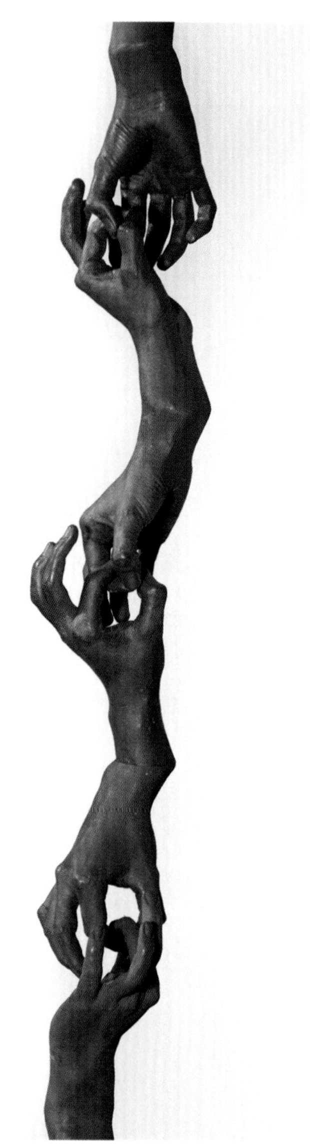

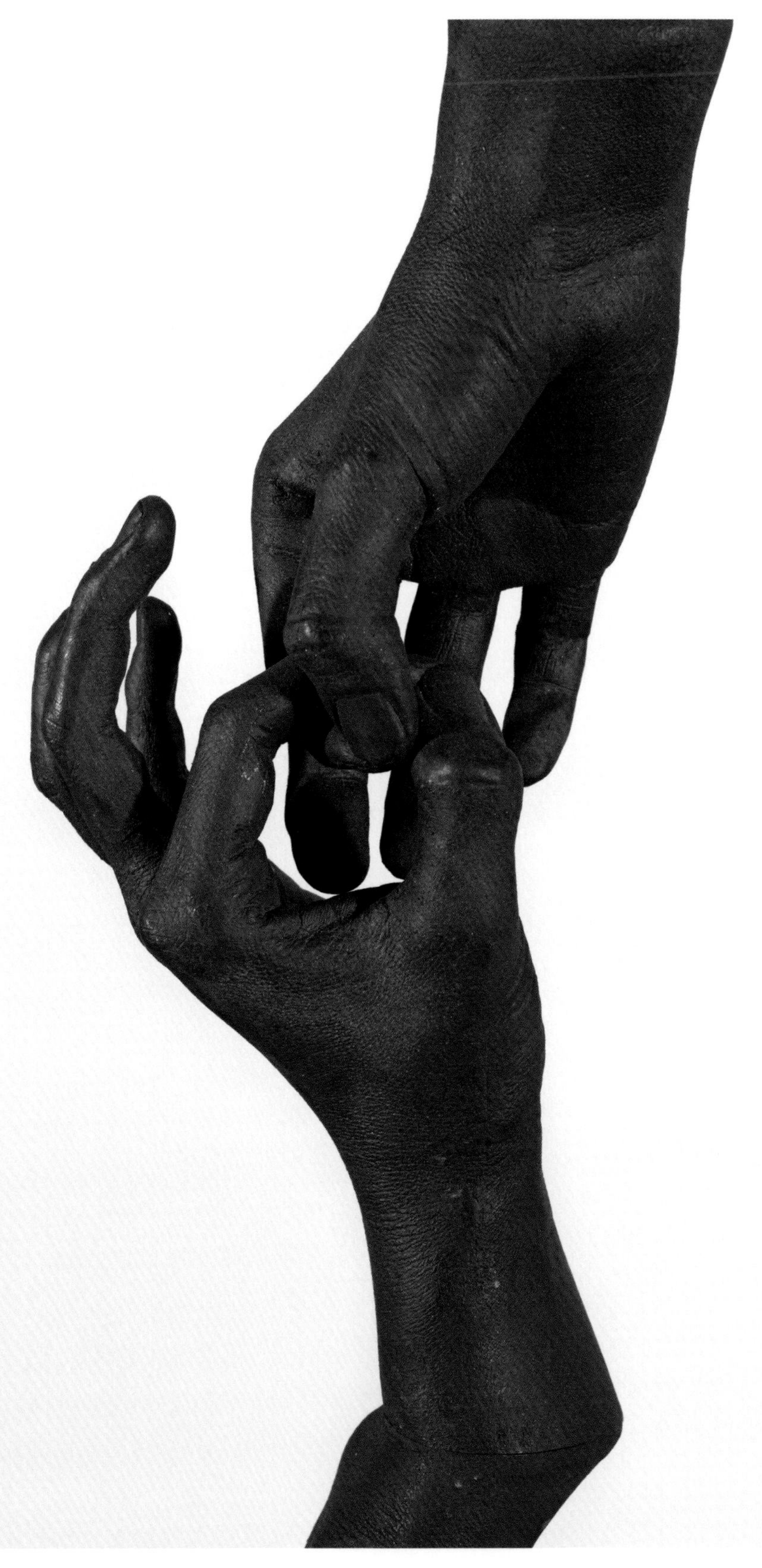

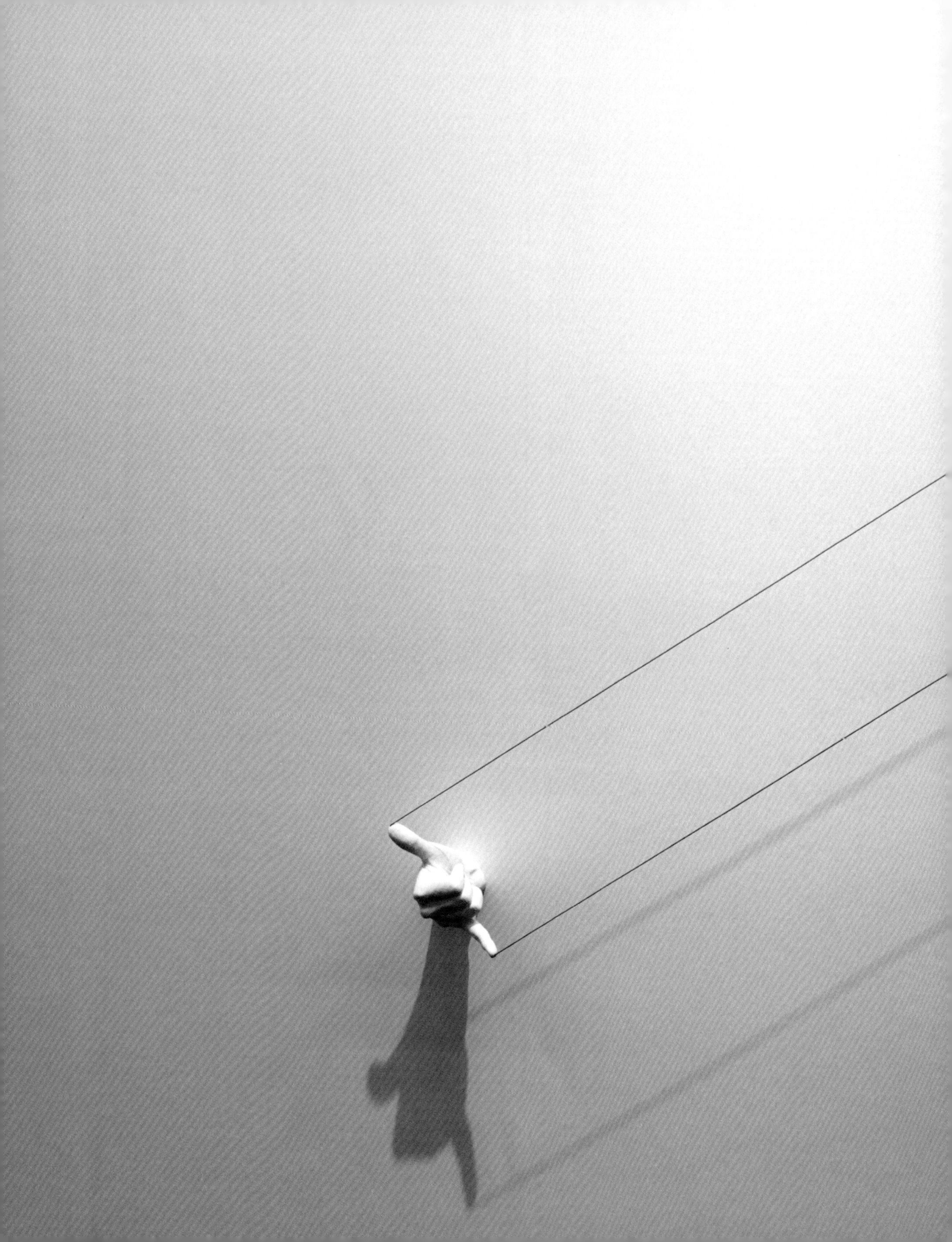

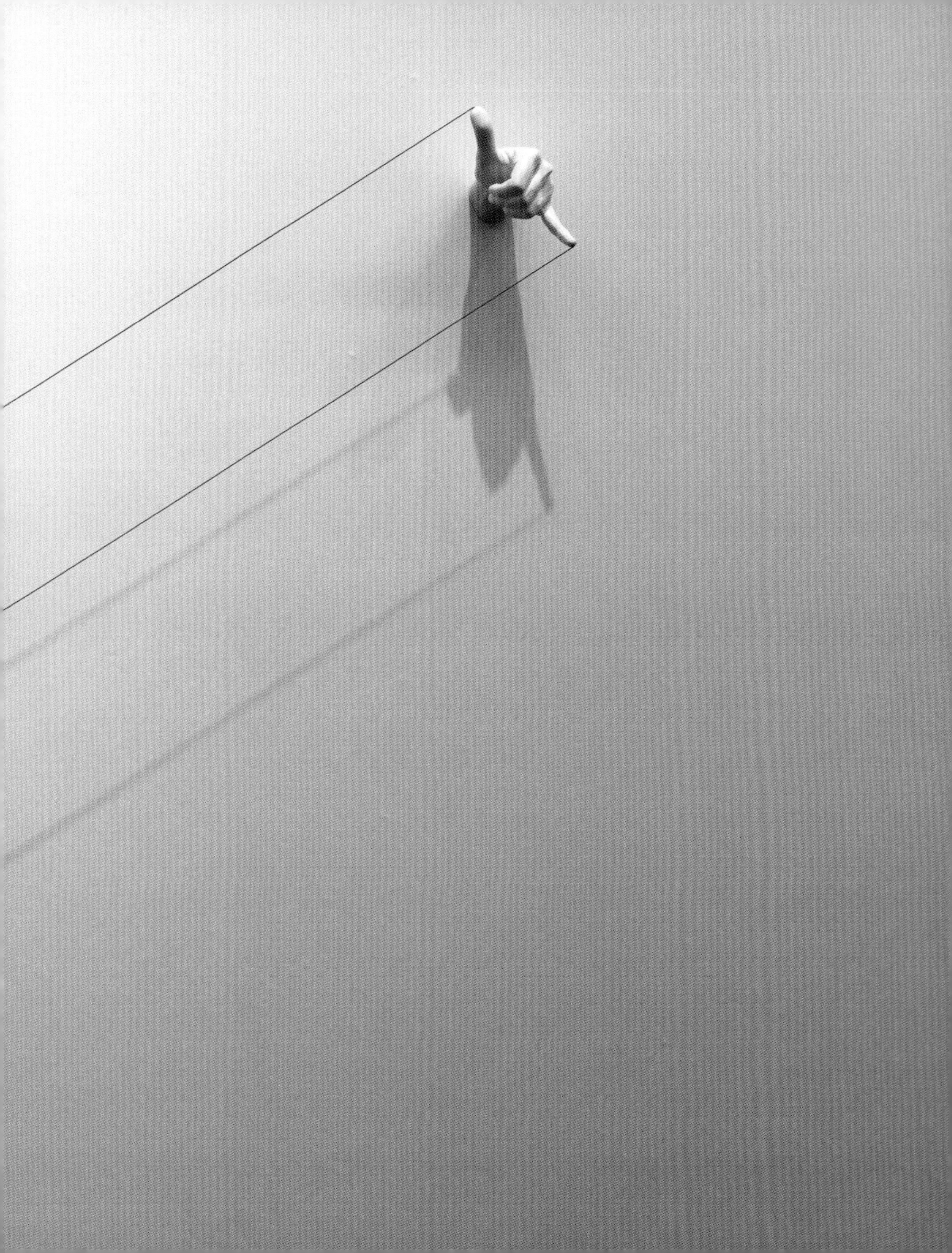

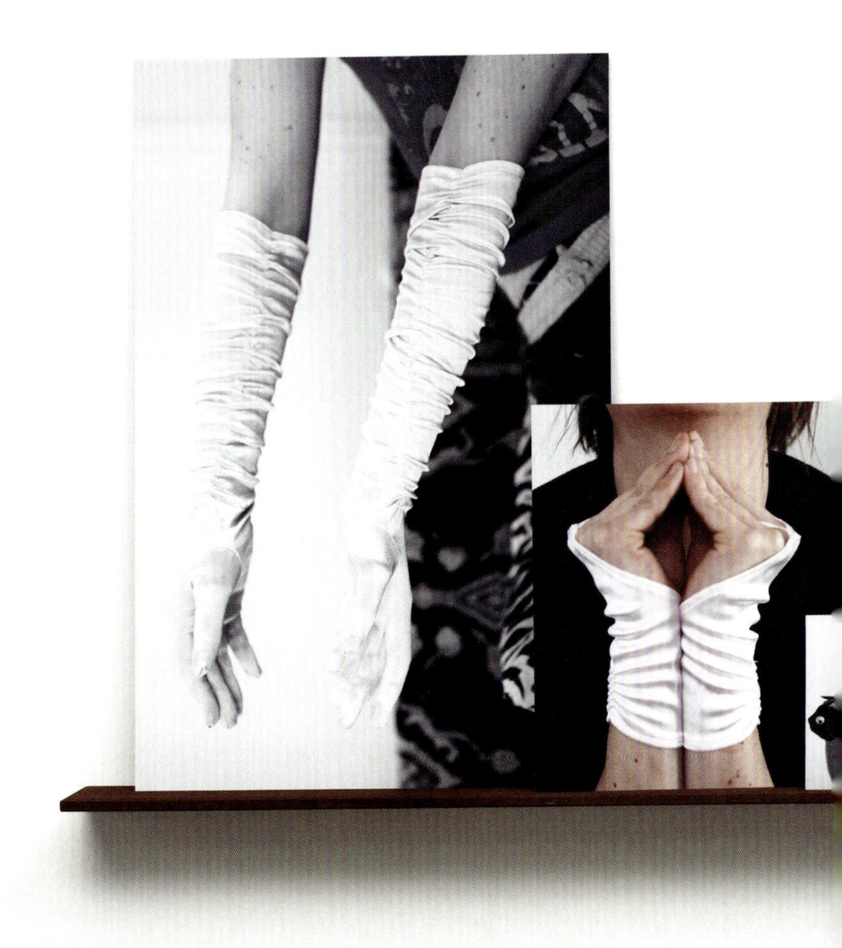

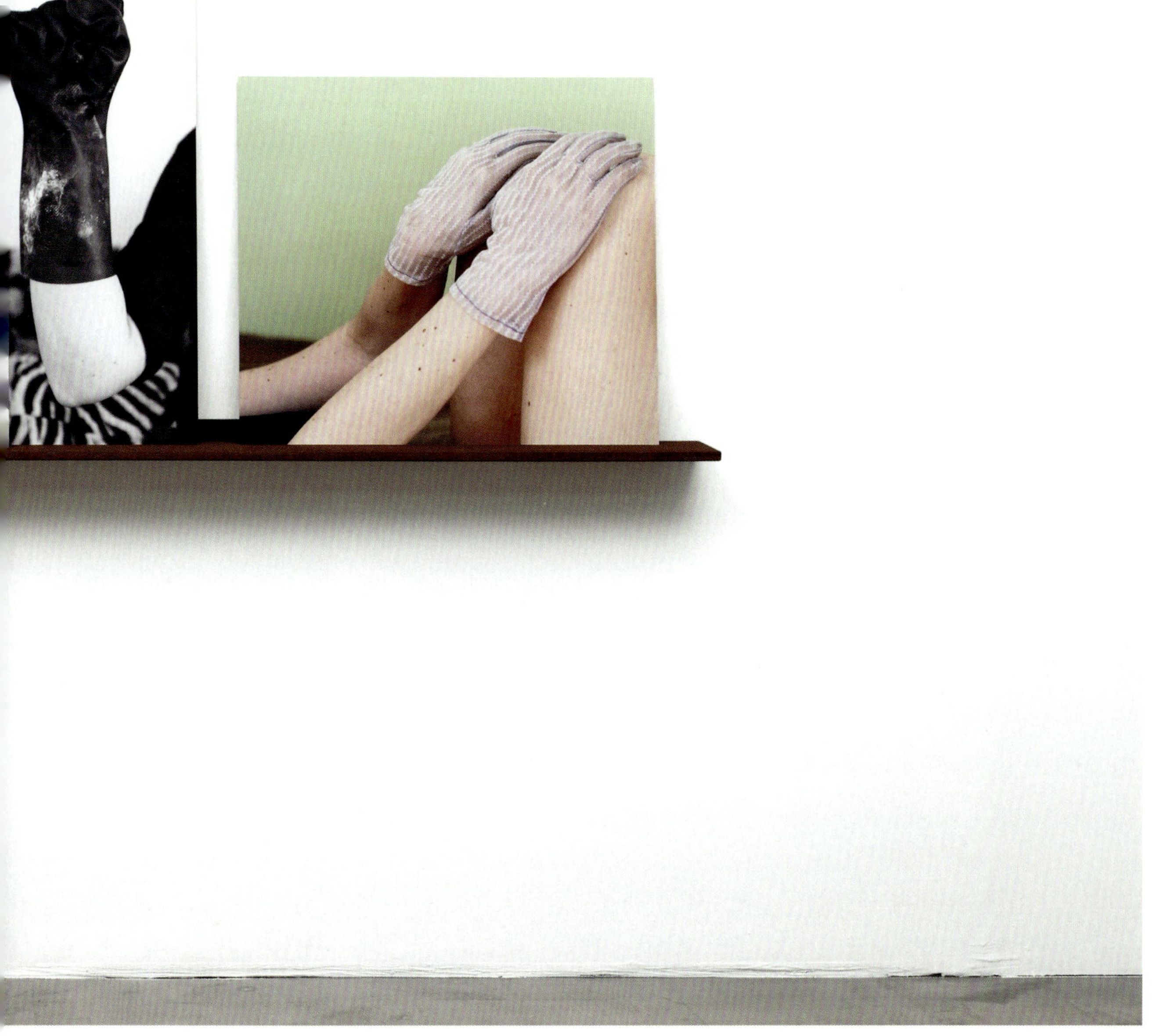

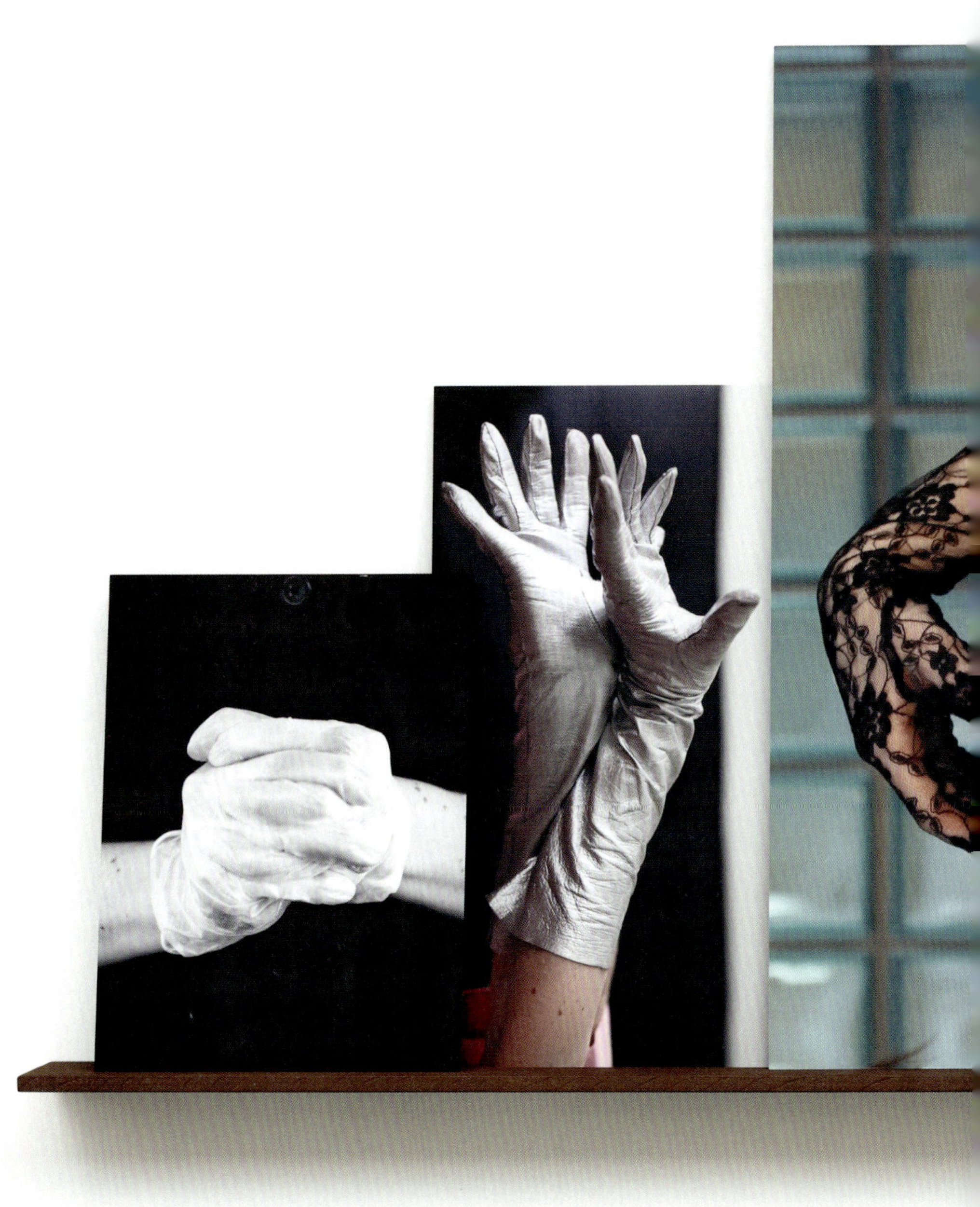

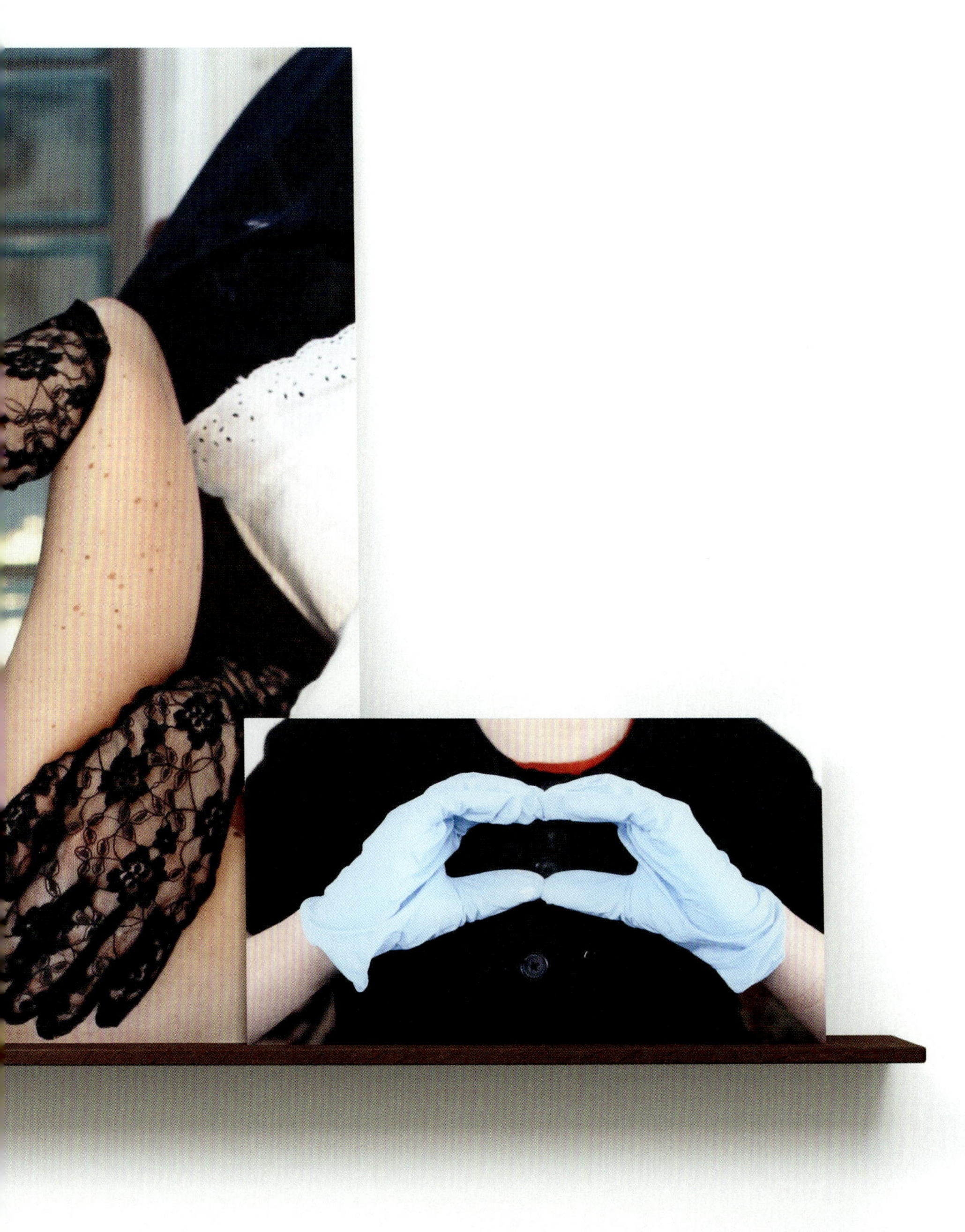

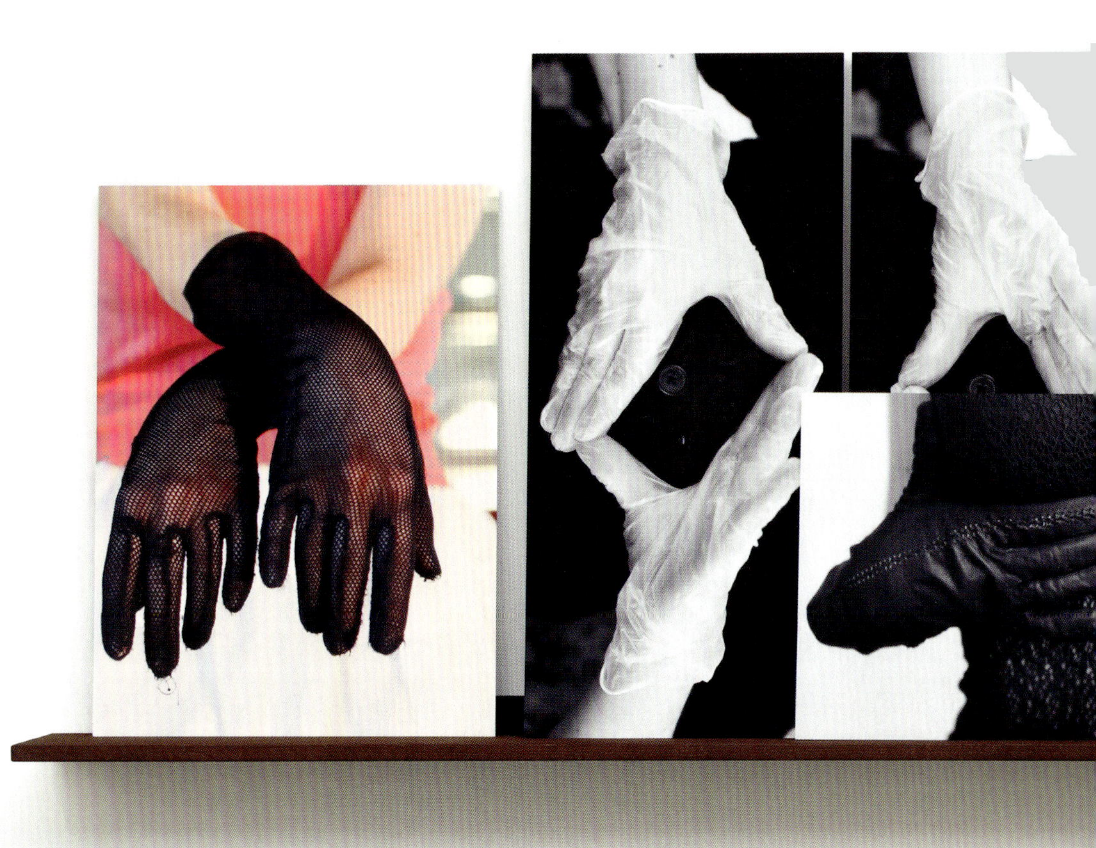

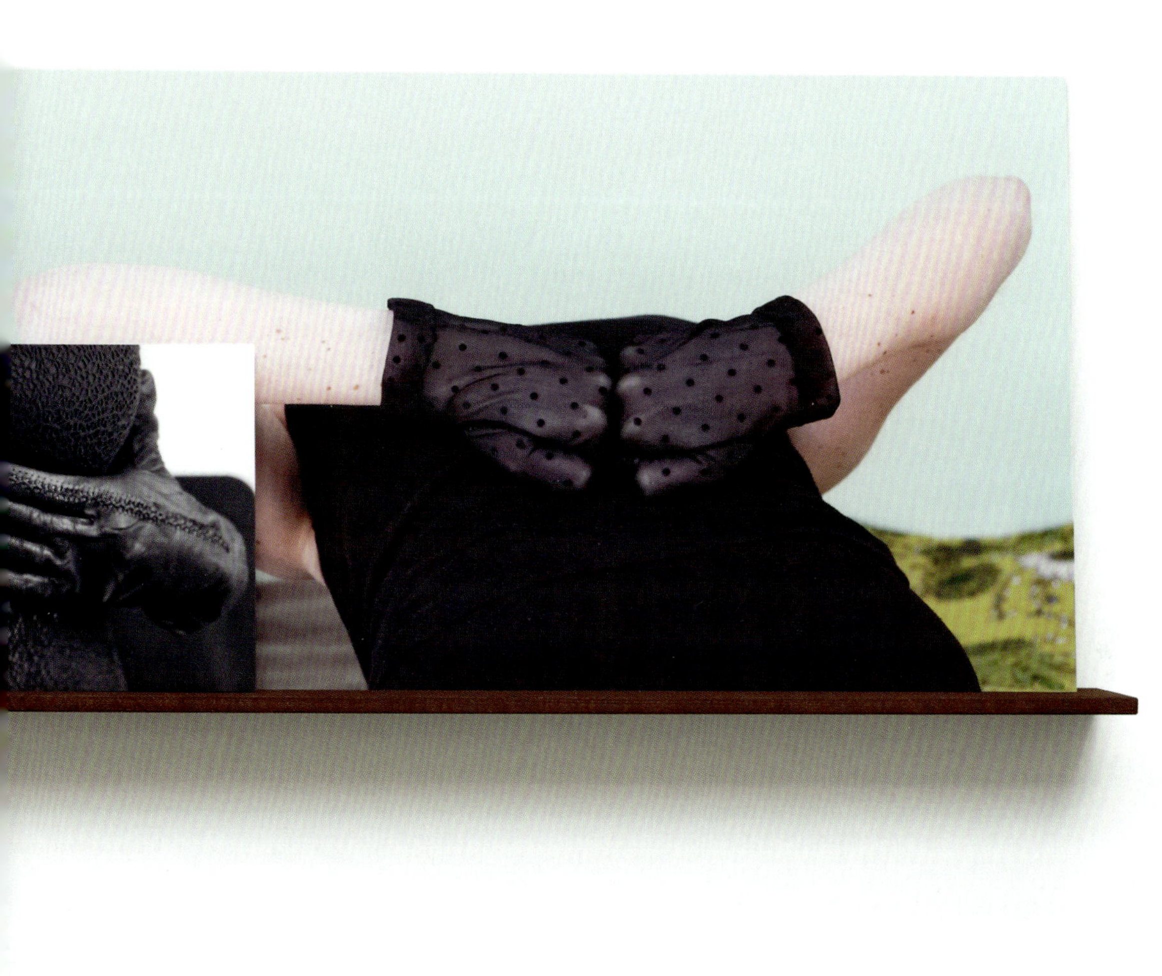

S. / pp. 62–63

CHANGING CONDITIONS, 2012
aluminium, powder coated, string
Ø 1,49 m

S. / pp. 64–69

GLOVES I, 2012
archival inkjet print on paper on MDF wood, oak board
286 x 125 x 15 cm
Installation COSAR HMT

GLOVES III
220 x 114 x 15 cm

GLOVES II
254 x 76 x 15 cm

S. / pp. 71–77

NANA, 2010–2011
ink, pencil and various objects on paper
framed, paper 90 x 74 cm
Installation KIT Düsseldorf

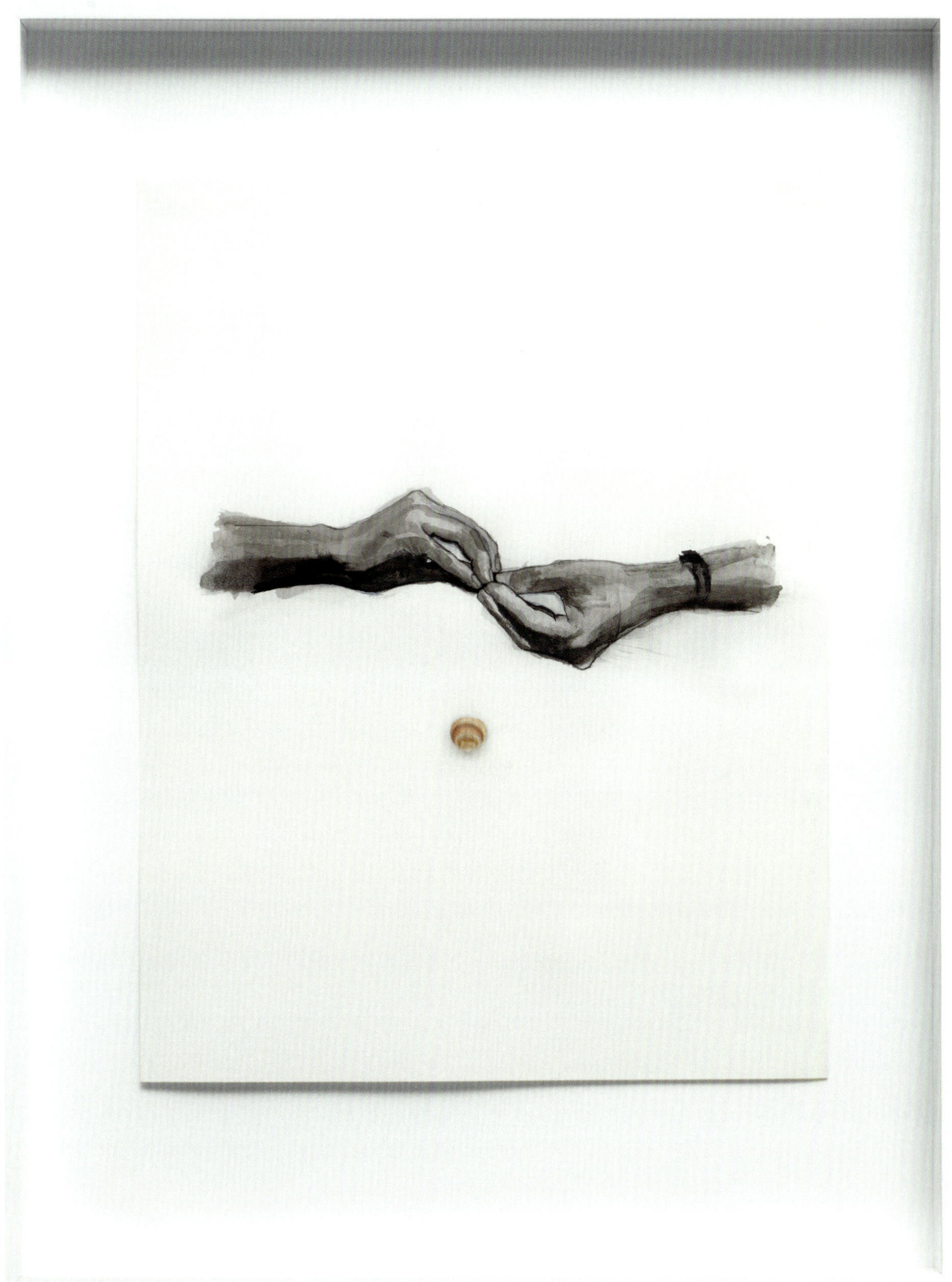

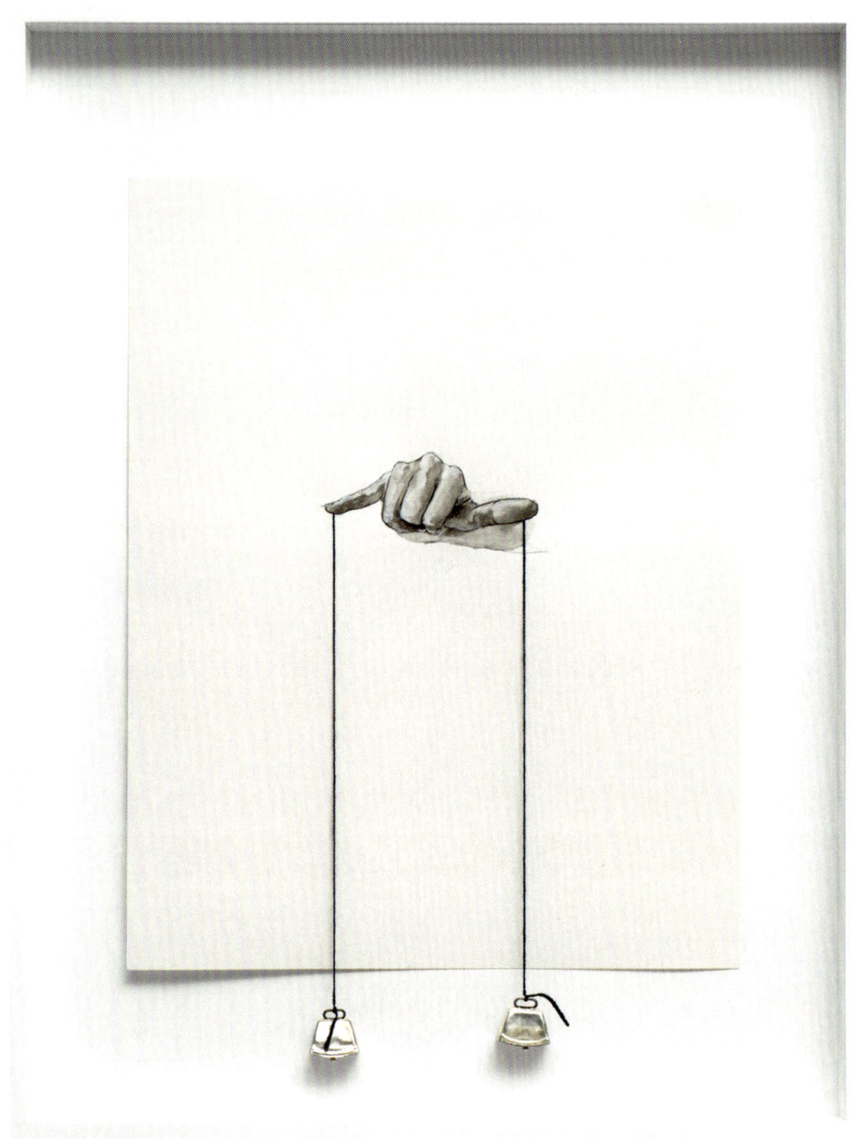

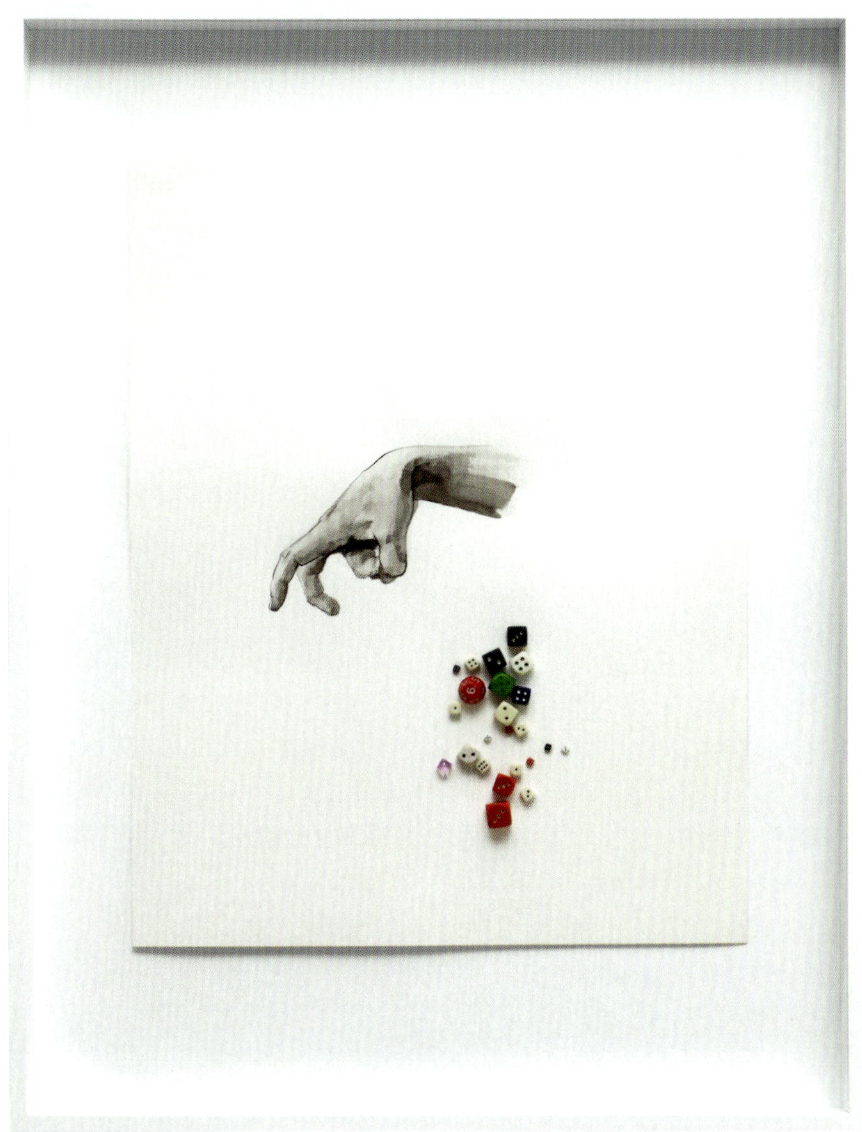

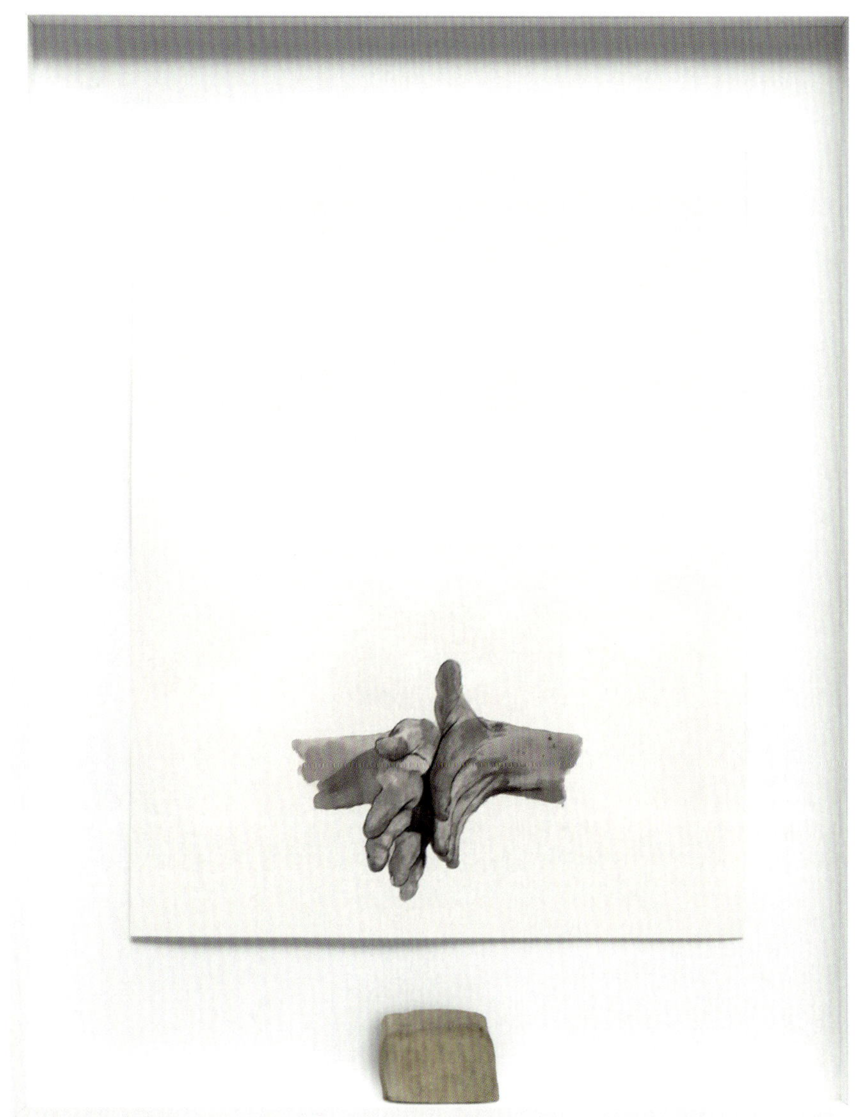

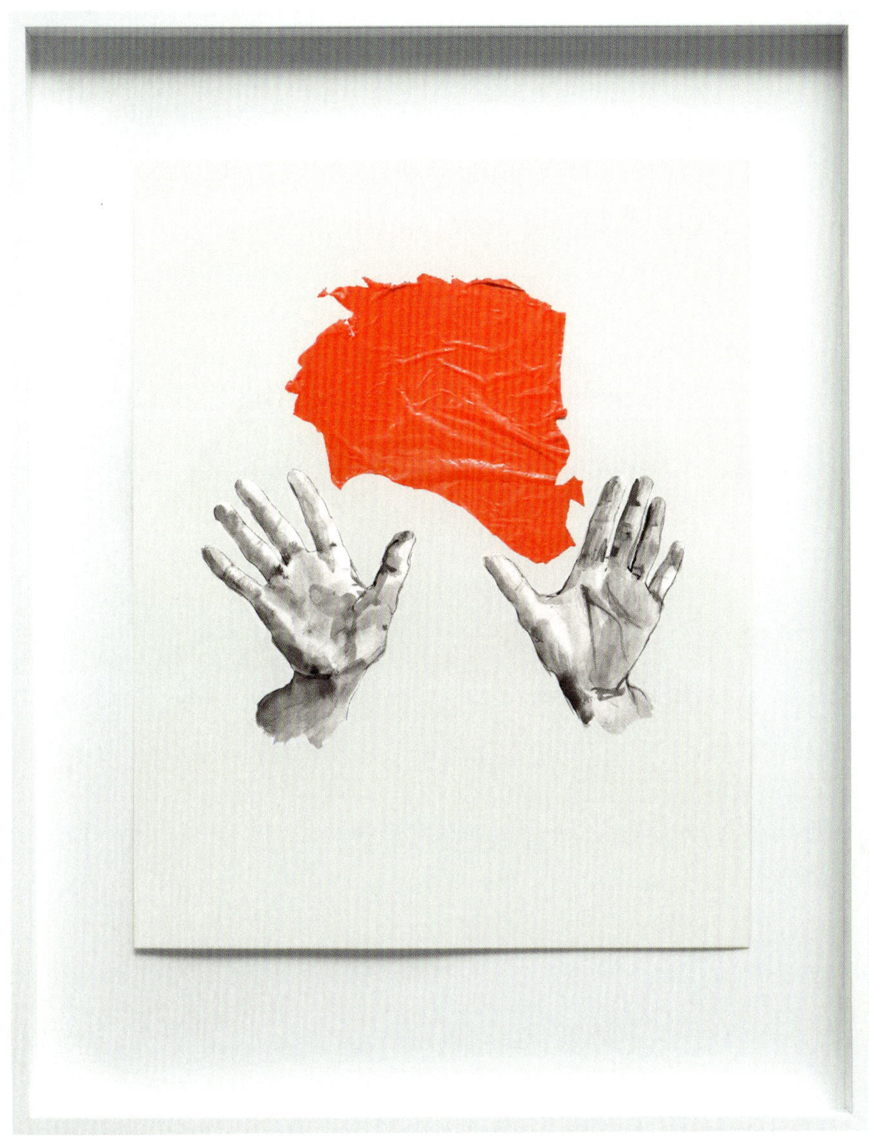

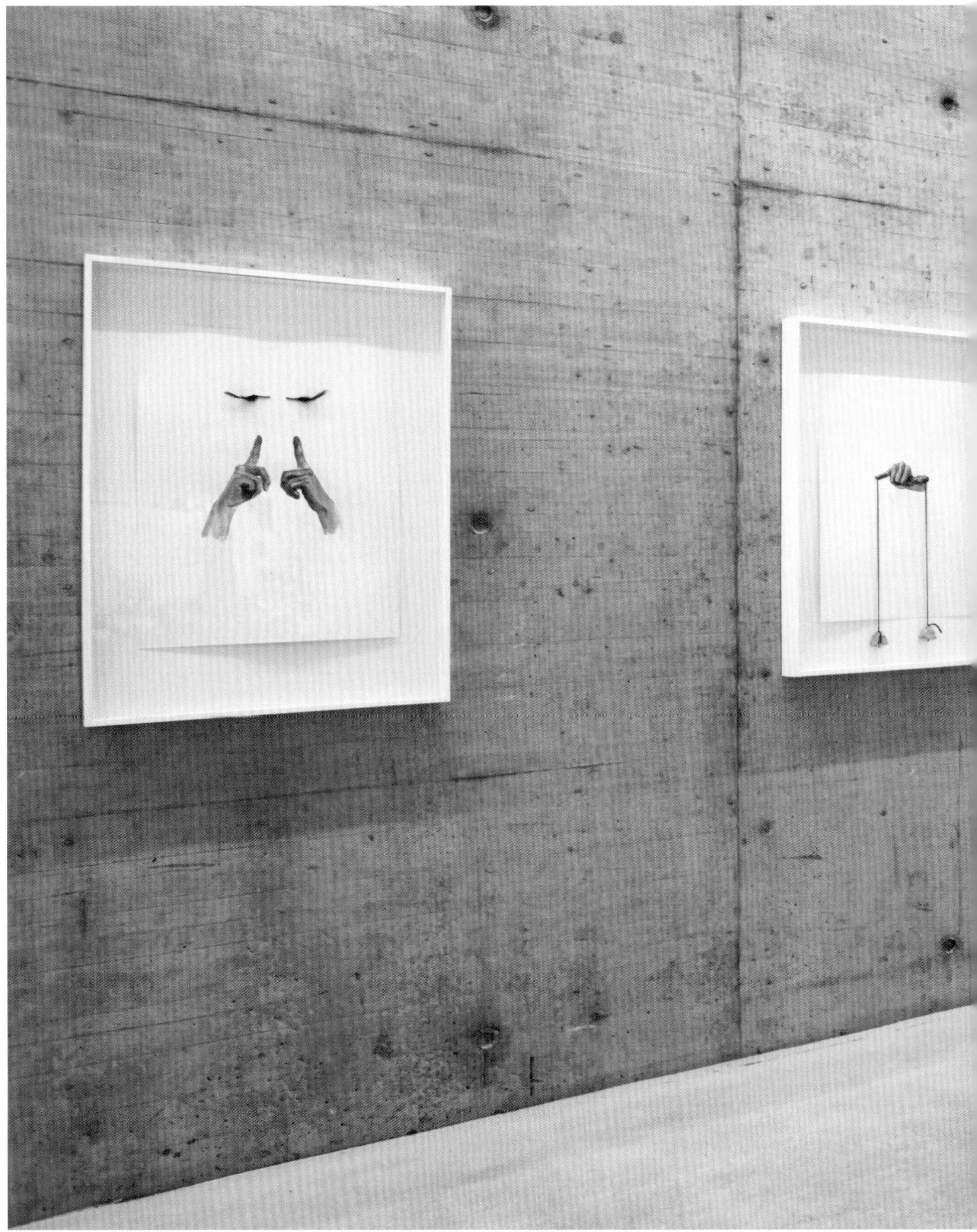

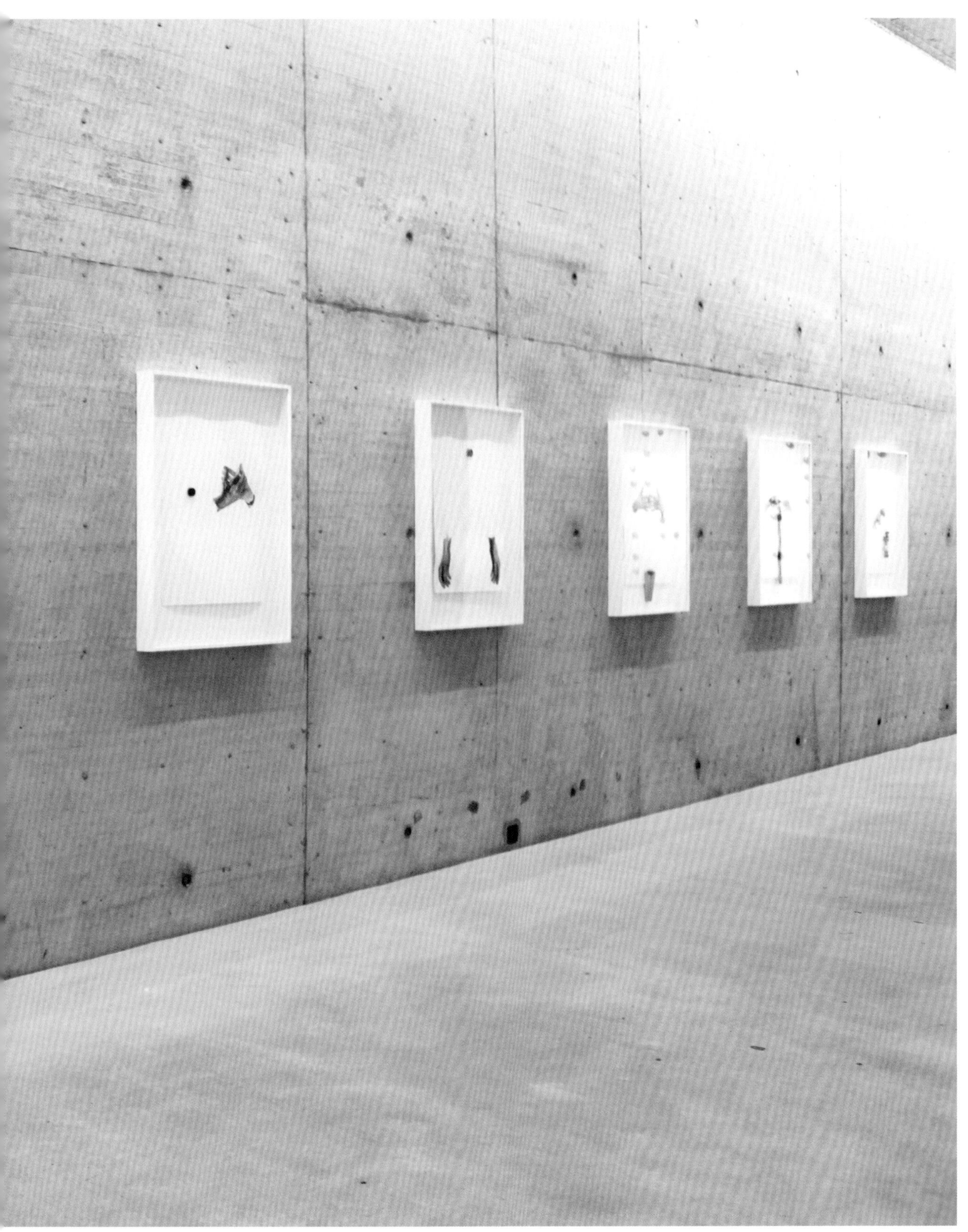

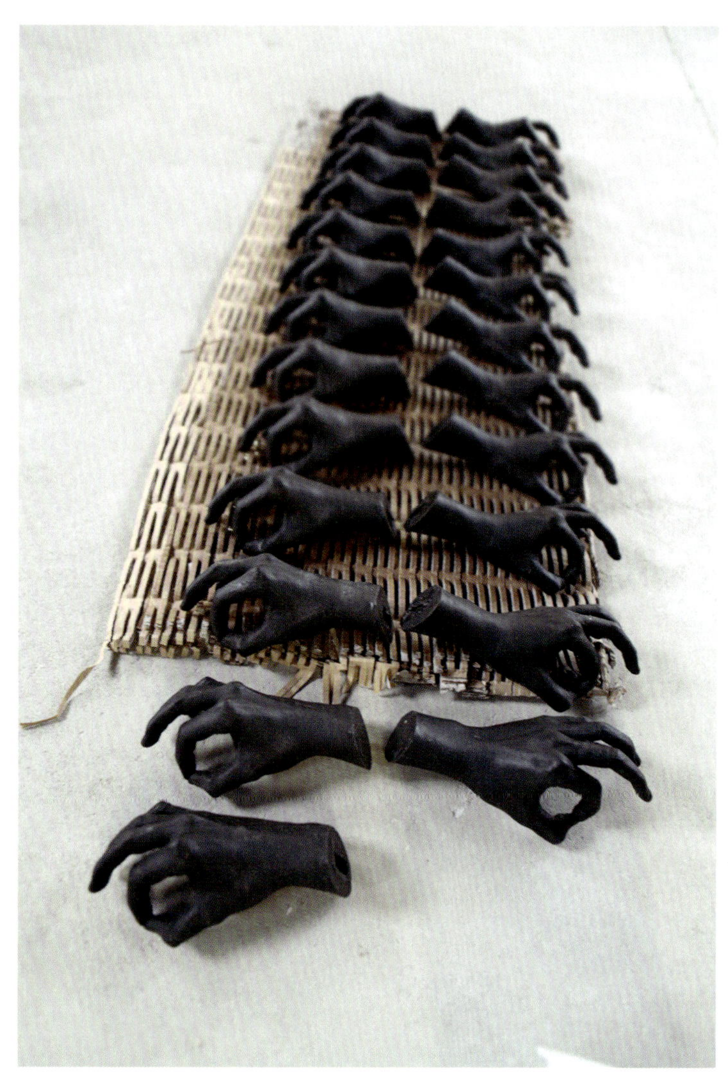

SLEEP SAVE, 2013
patinized bronze
115 x 47 x 2,5 cm

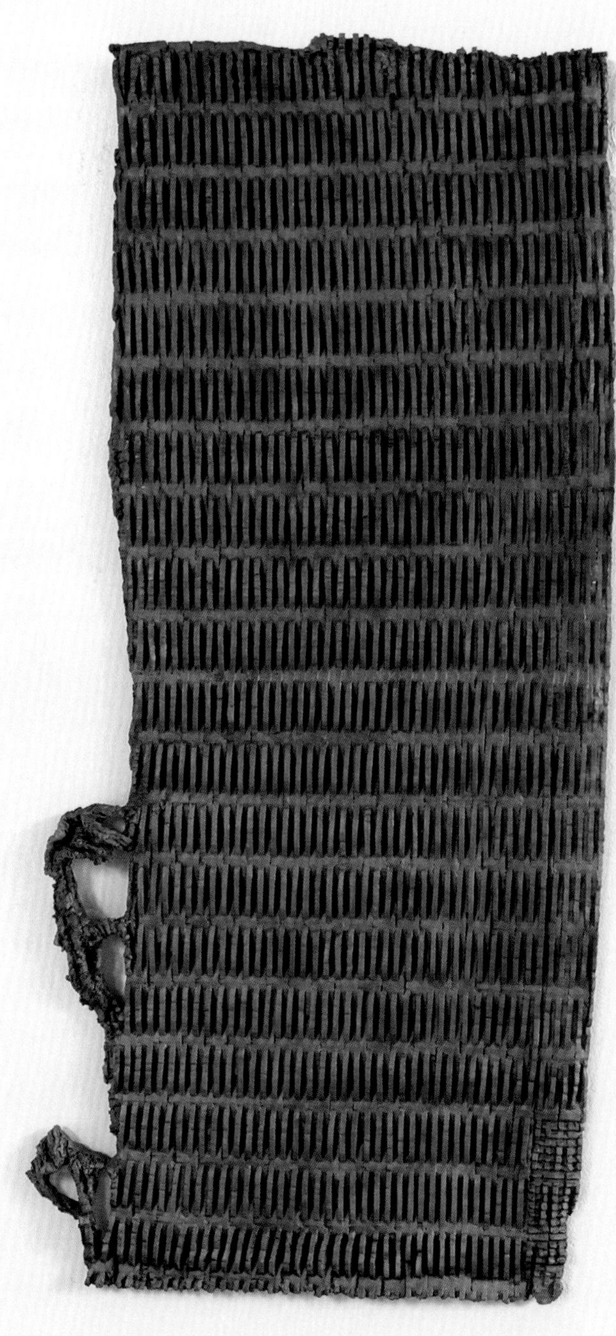

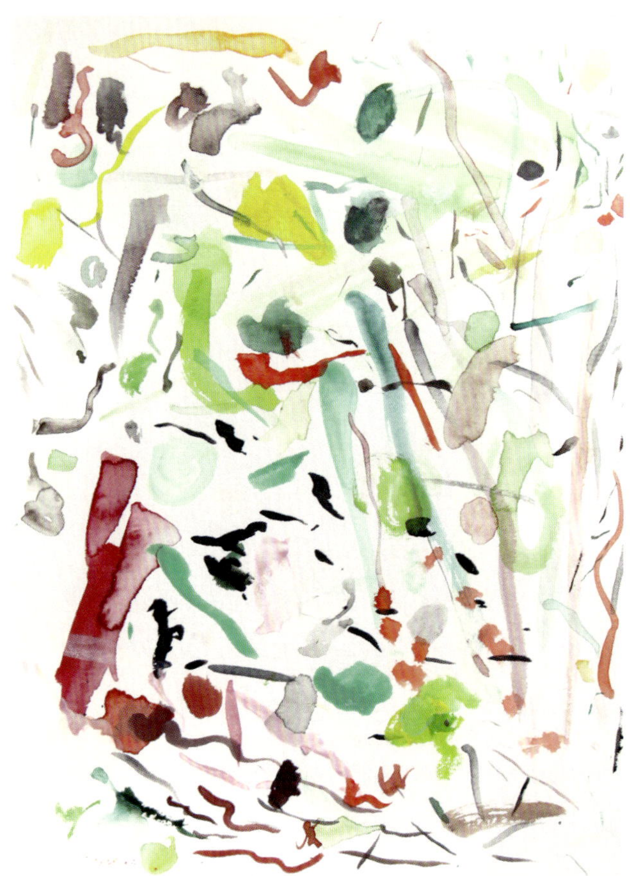

4 PAGES, 2013
watercolor, 14,7 x 21 cm

S. / pp. 82–83

SPUR, 2015
Dur plaster, 223 x 100 x 6 cm

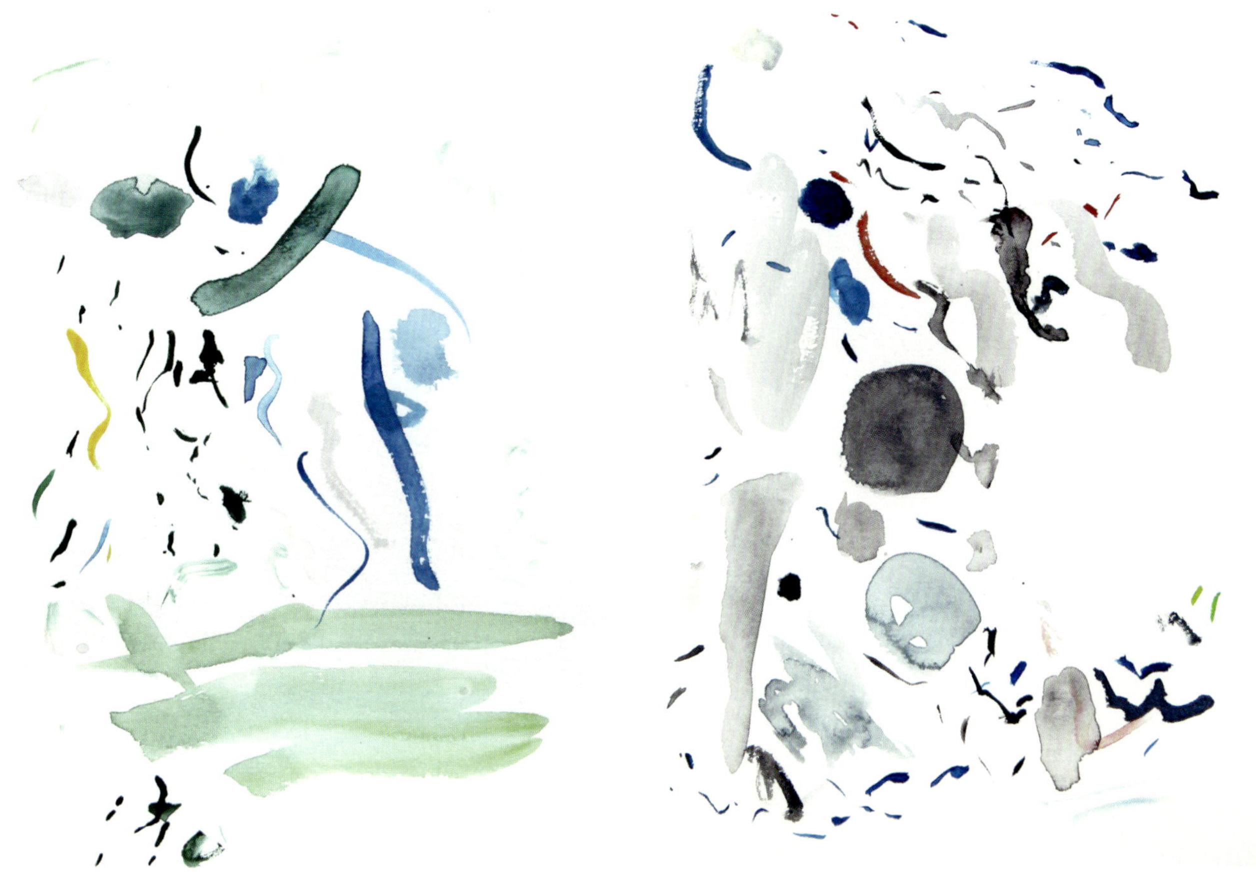

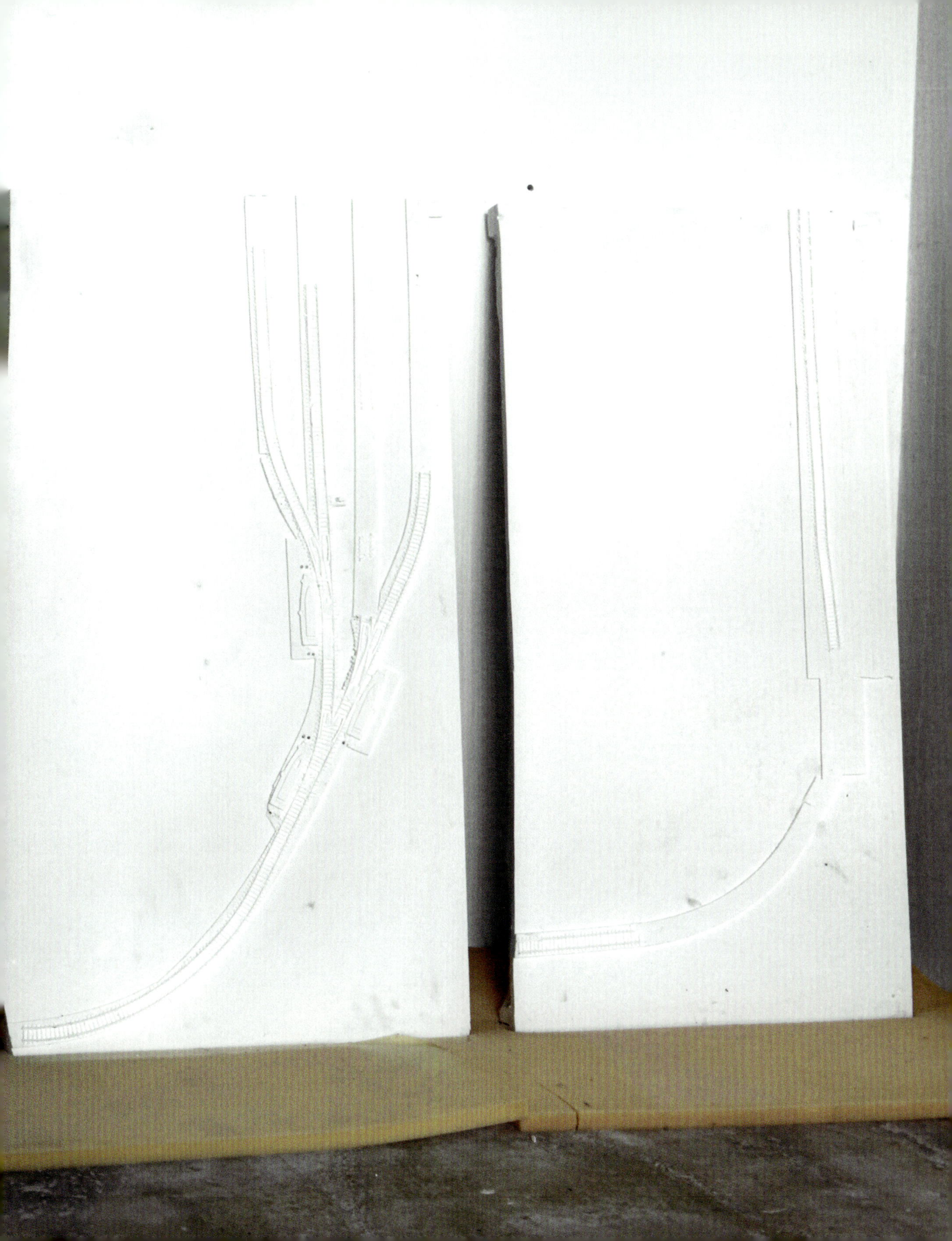

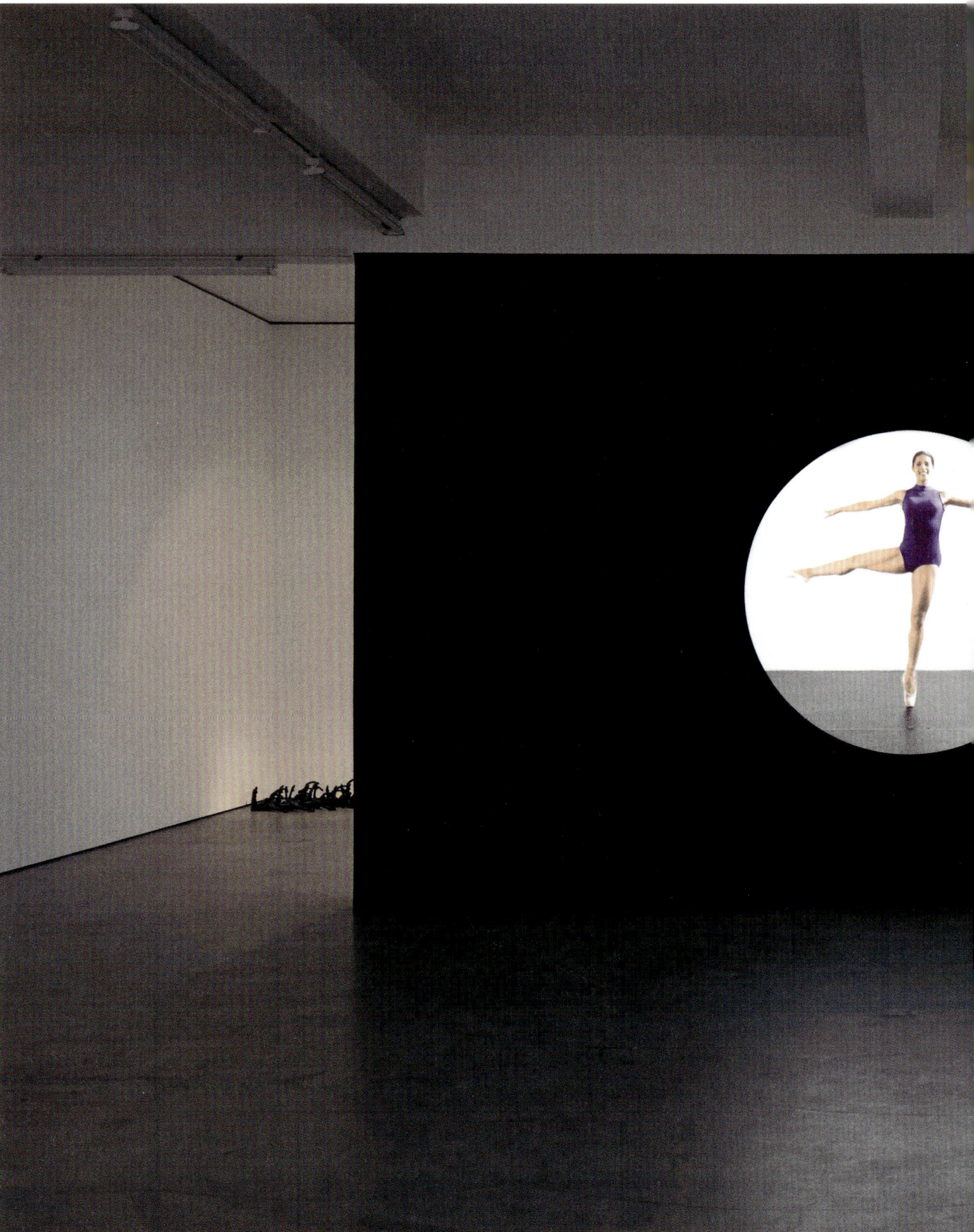

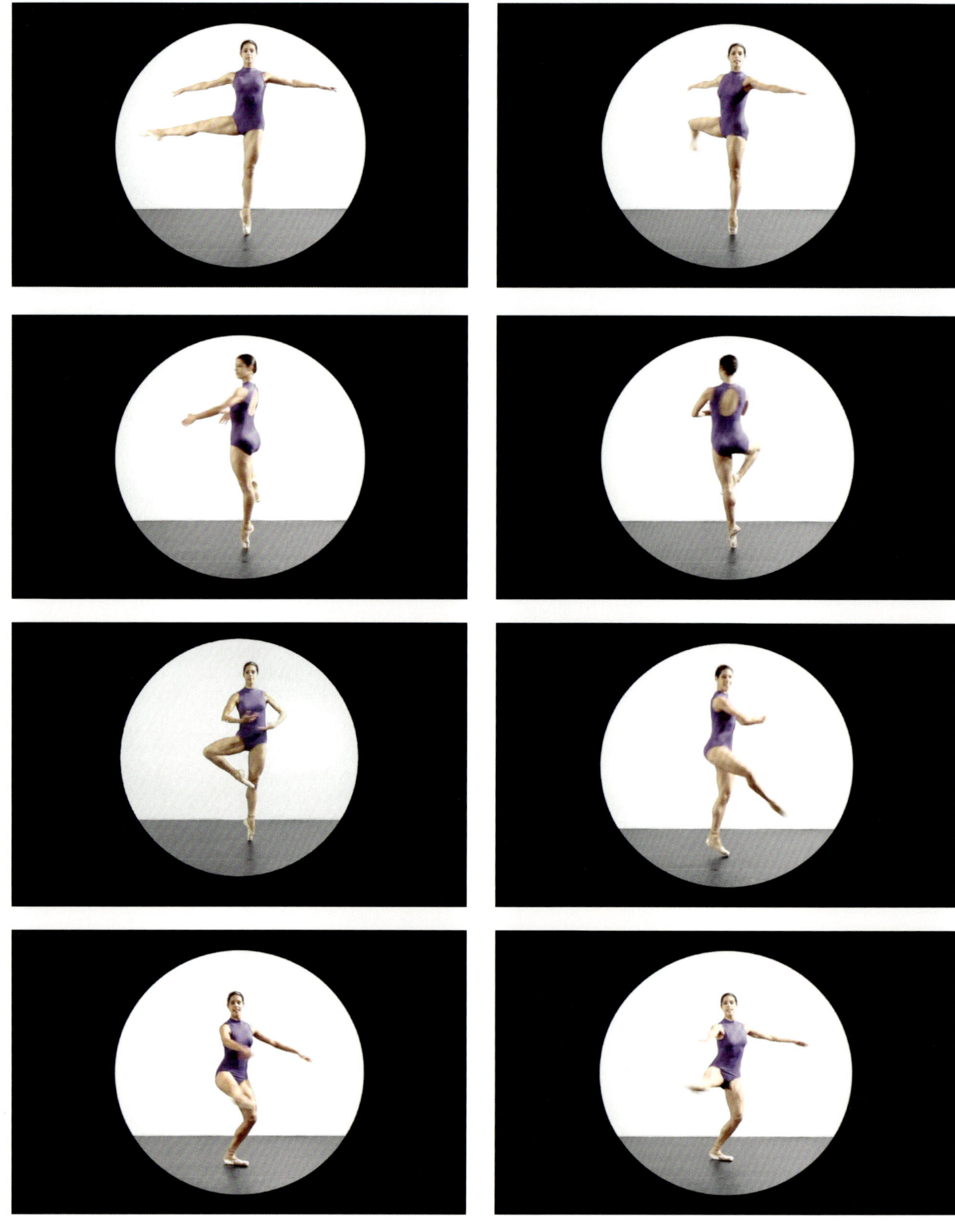

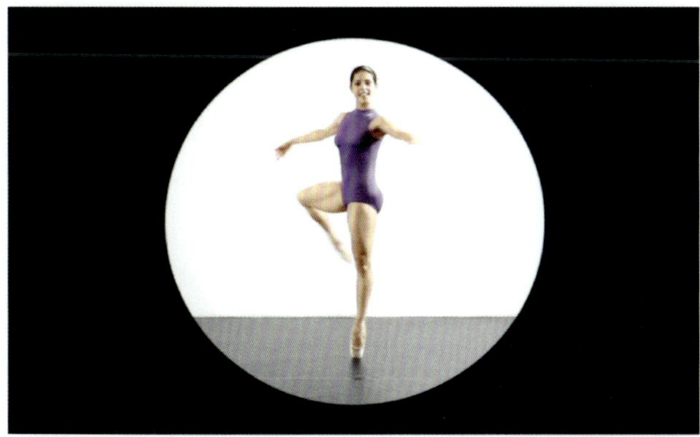

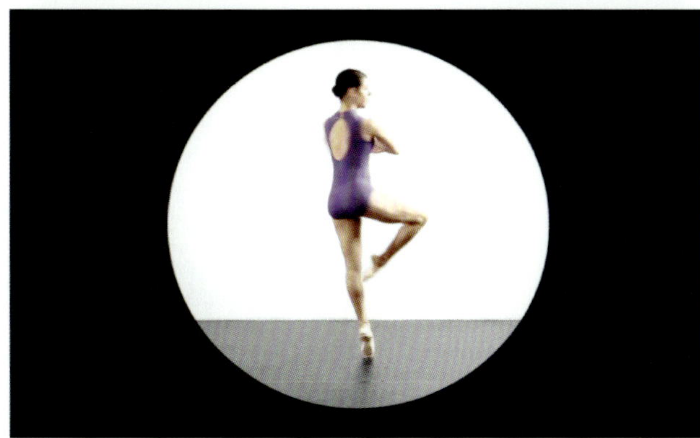

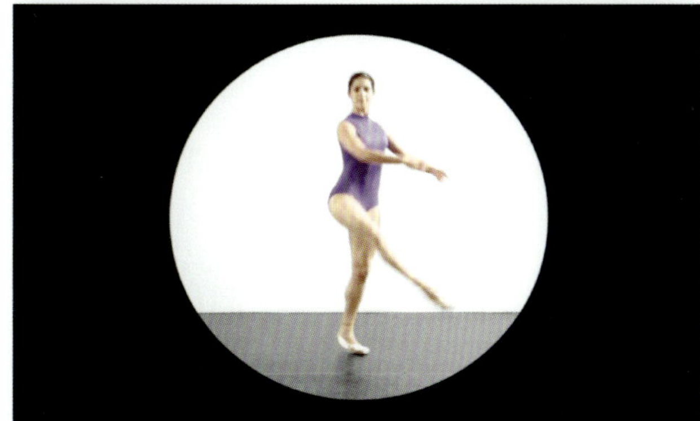

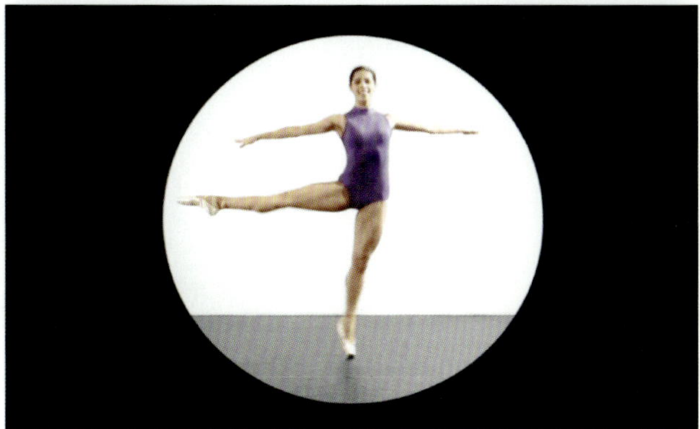

S. / pp. 84–87

32, 2010
projection Ø 1,80 m
color, loop
video installation COSAR HMT

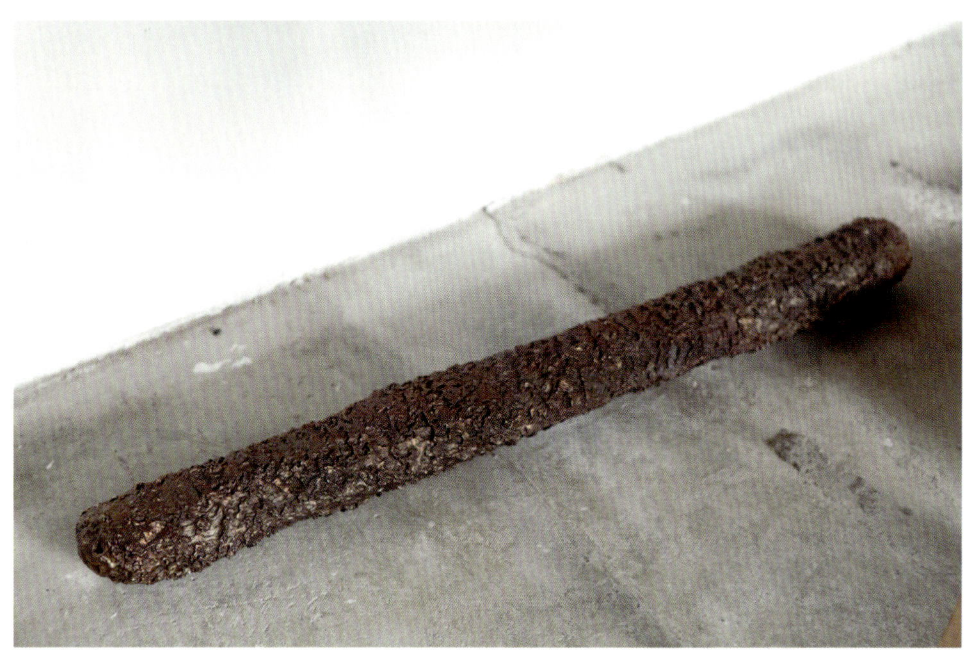

SHUT UP, 2014
patinized bronze
115 x 9,7 x 4,5 cm

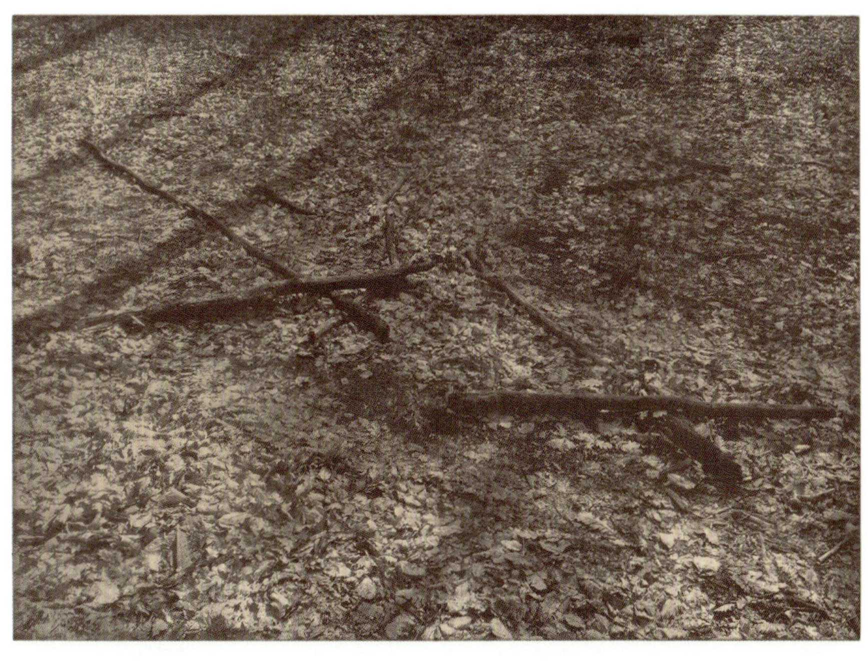

RAUTE (BRANDENBURG), 2014/2015
photogravure with bronze pigment on Buetten paper
55,7 x 66,5 cm, ed. of 8

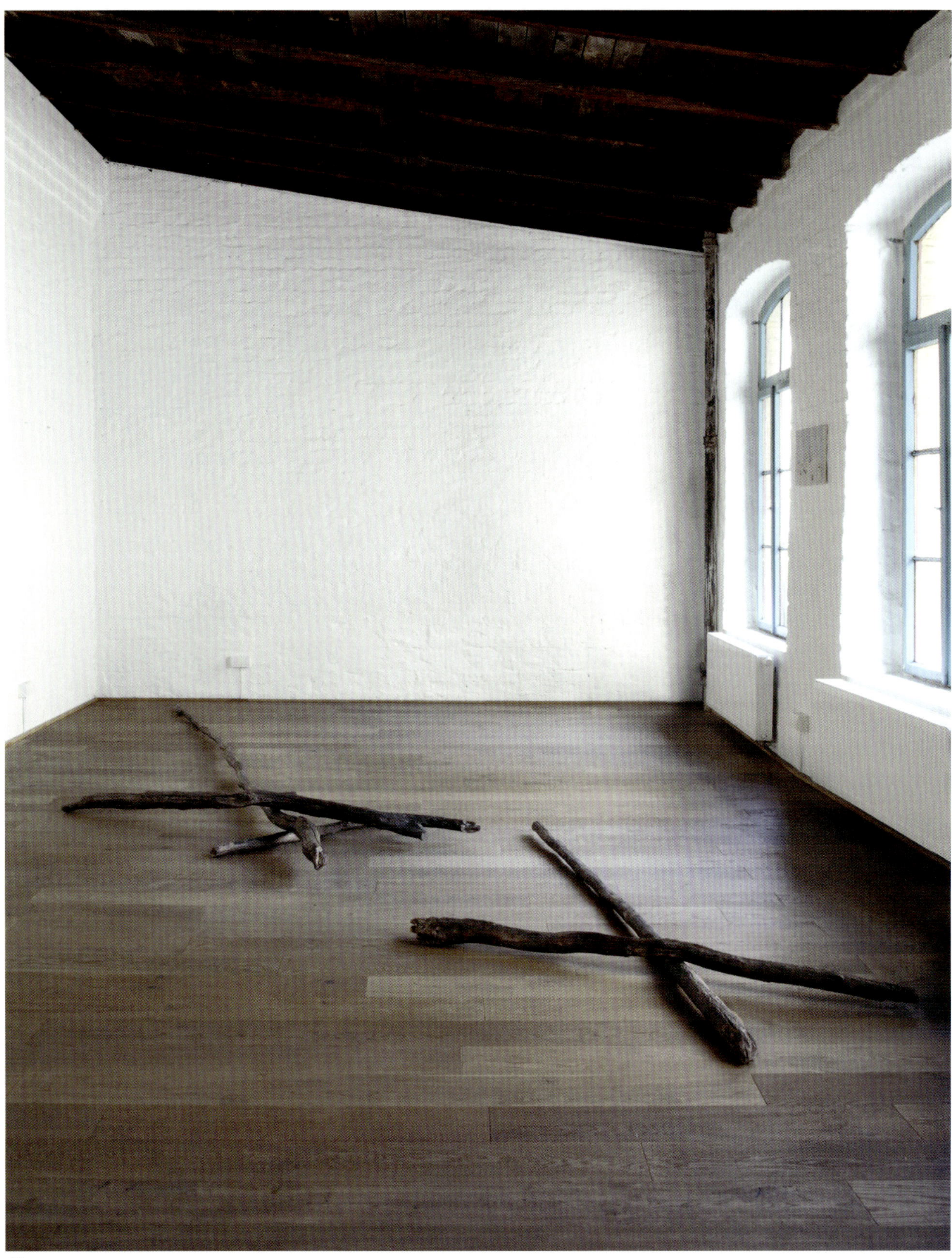

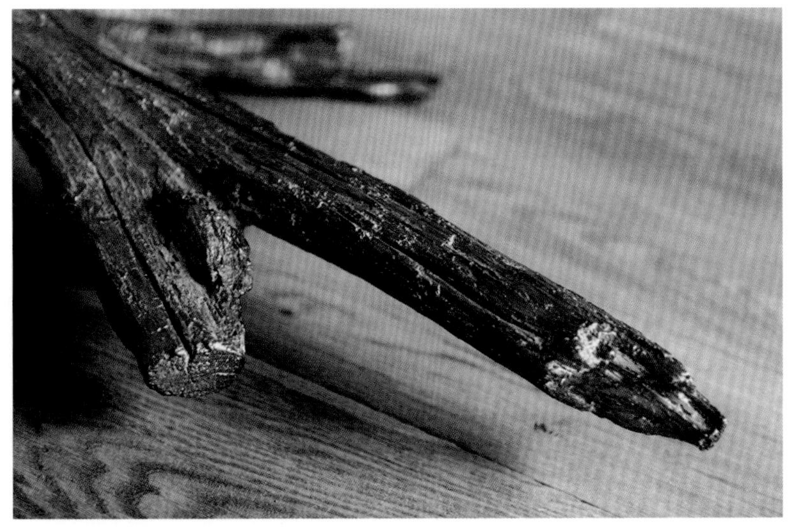

RAUTE (BRANDENBURG), 2014/2015
patinized bronze
664 x 225 x 21 cm
Installation Matthias Erntges Düsseldorf

BONE (FEUERWERKSKÖRPER), 2015
coppered bronze cast, 87 x 3 cm

BIOGRAFIE / BIOGRAPHY

Maren Maurer
*1981 in Scherzingen, Schweiz;
lebt in Köln / *1981 born in Scherzingen, Switzerland; lives in Cologne

AUSBILDUNG / EDUCATION
1998–2001 Akademie des Tanzes, Mannheim University of Music and Performing Arts
2002–2004 Burg Giebichenstein, University of Art and Design Halle/S.
Martin-Luther University Halle/S.
2005–2009 Staatliche Kunstakademie Düsseldorf

STIPENDIEN, PREISE / AWARDS, GRANTS
2011 Förderpreis NRW / award for emerging artists of the country North Rhine Westphalia
2009–2010 Bronner Artist-in-Residence Tel Aviv, Israel
2009 Art in the Office Award, AT Kearney

EINZELAUSSTELLUNGEN / SOLO EXHIBITIONS
2014 *Breathe Normally*, RAUM Oberkassel, Düsseldorf
2012 *Changing Conditions*, COSAR HMT Galerie, Düsseldorf
2010 *Maren Maurer*, COSAR HMT Galerie Düsseldorf
Falling Into Place, (mit / with Vera Lossau), Turm Kunstverein Konstanz
2009 *desks and tables*, RAUM Oberkassel, Düsseldorf

GRUPPENAUSSTELLUNGEN / GROUP EXHIBITIONS (AUSWAHL / SELECTION)
2015 *The Vacancy*, Kunsthaus Friedrichstraße, Galerie Crone, Berlin
Der erste Blick, Matthias Erntges Galerie, Düsseldorf
2014 *Der schwarze Hund*, Kunstverein Baden-Baden
Verhandlungstisch, Turm Kunstverein Konstanz
2012 *Bronner Residency: die Stipendiaten*, Kunst im Tunnel, Düsseldorf
2011 *Paper Framed Behind Glass*, COSAR HMT Galerie, Düsseldorf
Fields of Lawn (mit / with Vera Lossau), RAUM Oberkassel, Düsseldorf
Sunbeam in the Glasshouse, 701 E.V., Düsseldorf (K/C)
2010 *Think German*, German Embassy, London, UK
Singenkunst 2010, Museum Singen (K/C)
Regarding Düsseldorf 5, 701 E.V., Düsseldorf (K/C)
2009 *Jahresgaben*, Kunstverein für die Rheinlande und Westfalen, Düsseldorf (K/C)
Orders. Secrets. Embarrassments ... And Then We Start Again, General Public, Berlin
Fremdkörper, Orangerie Schloss Benrath
2008 *On Interchange*, Perfectural University of Fine Arts and Music, Aichi, JPN

PERFORMANCES
2015 *Chakrapeng!*, *Broken Spaces*, Kai 10, Düsseldorf
2012 Coperforming Discoteca Flaming Star, *Eigentlich 12 x Alissa*, Frankfurter Kunstverein
2010 *Presents*, Singenkunst 2010, Museum Singen (K/C)
Coperforming Joan Jonas' Reading *Dante II*, Julia Stoschek Collection, Düsseldorf
2009 *Ingrid (Inzwischen)* mit / with Discoteca Flaming Star, Performa 09, New York City, USA
for boris for ingrid mit / with Discoteca Flaming Star, Kunstverein Harburger Bahnhof, Hamburg
2008 *A Gleam of Dust*, Cluster Arts Magazine Event, London, UK
A Performance on Lust and Transformation, Niu Gallery, Barcelona, ES
Buchprojekt *Sunbird and Gloria* mit / with Mark von Schlegell, Glen Rubsamen, u. a. / et al
Mary Around The Tree, 'One-Night-Stand' Event (mit / with Rita McBride), 5. Berlin Biennale, KW Kunstwerke, Berlin
Die Stimmung unsrer Seelen (mit / with Klara Adam)
'WG/3ZI/K/BAR' Jakobihaus, Malkasten Künstlerverein, Düsseldorf
Even a plaster bird needs to practice, workshop mit / with Joan Jonas, Barcelona, ES
With a Pokerface, Stadtmuseum Hattingen (mit / with Vera Lossau)
Ab / Since 2007 *New Tribune Performance Reel* (mit / with Rita McBride, Manuel Graf, Discoteca Flaming Star), Malkasten Künstlerverein, Düsseldorf, Artforum Art Fair Berlin, General Public Berlin

BARBARA KÖNCHES studierte Philosophie, Wirtschaftswissenschaften, Kunst- und Technikgeschichte in Trier und Karlsruhe und promovierte 2000 im Fach Philosophie.
Bis 2006 war sie Leiterin der Videosammlung und Kuratorin am ZKM/ Zentrum für Kunst und Medientechnologie Karlsruhe sowie Leiterin des Internationalen Medienpreises in Kooperation mit dem Südwestrundfunk Baden-Baden.
Neben ihrer Ausstellungs- und Symposienreihe „Kunst und Philosophie" für den Projektraum des ZKM publizierte sie u. a. *Ethik und Ästhetik der Werbung. Phänomenologie eines Skandals* (Frankfurt: Lang, 2001), und mit Peter Weibel (Hrsg.), *UnSICHTBARes. Algorithmen als Schnittstelle zwischen Kunst und Wissenschaft* (Bern: Benteli, 2005).
Seit 2007 ist sie Fachbereichsleiterin Visuelle Kunst bei der Kunststiftung NRW, Düsseldorf. Außerdem hat sie die künstlerische Gesamtleitung des Nam June Paik Awards inne. Sie konzipiert und leitet Ausstellungsinitiativen und publiziert.

BARBARA KÖNCHES studied philosohpy, art and technology history and economic sciences in Trier and Karlsruhe. In 2000 she received her PhD in philosophy.
Until 2006 she then was head of the video collection as well as curator at ZKM / Center for Art and Media in Karlsruhe, leading the International Media Art Award in cooperation with Southwest Broadcasting, Baden-Baden.
As well as managing the exhibitions and symposia row for the project space of ZKM entitled "Art and Philosophy" she published i.a. *Ethik und Ästhetik der Werbung. Phänomenologie eines Skandals* (Frankfurt: Lang, 2001), and with Peter Weibel (ed.), *UnSICHTBARes. Algorithmen als Schnittstelle zwischen Kunst und Wissenschaft* (Bern: Benteli, 2005).
Since 2007 she is team supervisor of the Visual Art Departementat Kunststiftung NRW in Düsseldorf. Also she is the artistic manager of Nam June Paik Award. She conceptualizes and directs exhibition projects and publishes.

DORIS KRYSTOF ist Kunsthistorikerin, Autorin und Kuratorin bei der Kunstsammlung Nordrhein-Westfalen, Düsseldorf.
Nach dem Studium der Literaturwissenschaften, Geschichte und Kunstgeschichte in Freiburg/B. und Köln promovierte sie in Kunstgeschichte. Sie war als Kuratorin für moderne und zeitgenössische Kunst an der Kunstsammlung Nordrhein-Westfalen in Düsseldorf sowie der Kunsthalle Wien tätig und ist seit 2001 Kuratorin im K21 der Kunstsammlung Nordrhein-Westfalen in Düsseldorf.
Zu den von ihr kuratierten Einzelausstellungen gehören u. a. *Steve McQueen* (2001, Kunsthalle Wien), *Heimo Zobernig* (2003, K21 mit dem Mumok Wien und der Kunsthalle Basel), *Martin Kippenberger* (2006, K21 mit der Tate Modern, London), *Eija-Liisa Ahtila* (2008, K21 mit Jeu de Paume, Paris), *Jorge Pardo* (2009, K21), *Ana Torfs* (2010, K21 mit der Generali Foundation, Wien), *Gillian Wearing* (2012, K20 mit der Whitechapel Gallery London) und *Wael Shawky* (2014, K20). Zu den von ihr kuratierten Gruppenausstellungen zählen u. a. *Das ich ist etwas Anderes* (2000, K20), *40jahrevideokunst.de – Teil 1, Digitales Erbe: Videokunst in Deutschland von 1963 bis heute* (2006, K21), *Talking Pictures. Theatralität in zeitgenössischen Film- und Videoarbeiten* (2007, K21) sowie *Big Picture I–III* (2011–2012, K21).

DORIS KRYSTOF is an art historian, author and curator at Kunstsammlung Nordrhein-Westfalen in Düsseldorf.
After studying art history, literature and history at the Universities of Freiburg and Cologne and receiving a PhD in art history she worked as a curator for modern and contemporary art at K20 Düsseldorf, Kunsthalle Wien and since 2001 at the K21 in Düsseldorf.
Previous exhibitions include monographic shows of *Steve McQueen* (2001, Kunsthalle Wien), *Heimo Zobernig* (2003, K21 with Mumok Wien and Kunsthalle Basel), *Martin Kippenberger* (2006, K21 with Tate Modern, London), *Eija-Liisa Ahtila* (2008, K21 with Jeu de Paume, Paris), *Jorge Pardo* (2009, K21), *Ana Torfs* (2010, K21 with Generali Foundation, Wien), *Gillian Wearing* (2012, K20 with Whitechapel Gallery London), and *Wael Shawky* (2014, K20). Group shows include *The Self is something else* (2000, K20), *40jahrevideokunst.de* (2006, K21), *Talking Pictures - Theatricality in Contemporary Film and Video Art* (2007, K21), and *Big Picture I-III* (2011–2012, K21).

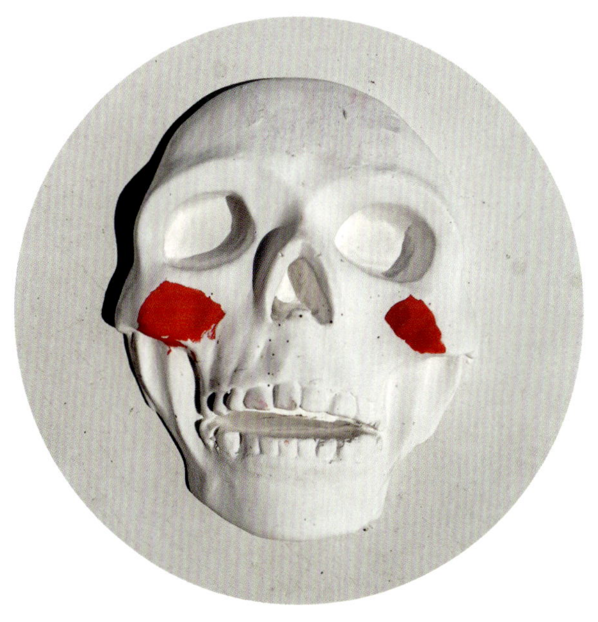

NO TITLE, 2014
plaster, watercolor
12 x 11 x 3 cm

IMPRESSUM / IMPRINT

Gestaltung / Design
Adeline Morlon

Texte / Texts
Barbara Könches (S. / pp. 25–26),
Doris Krystof (S. / pp. 47–51)

Übersetzungen / Translations
Jeremy Gaines (S. / pp. 28–31, S. / pp. 53–57)

Lektorat / Copy-Editing
Iris Seemann

Lithografie / Image Editing
bildarbeit, Henning Krause

Produktion / Production Management
DISTANZ, Sonja Bahr

Gesamtherstellung / Production
optimal media GmbH, Röbel/Müritz

Vertrieb / Distribution
Gestalten, Berlin
www.gestalten.com
sales@gestalten.com

ISBN 978-3-95476-128-9
Printed in Germany

Erschienen im / Published by
DISTANZ Verlag
www.distanz.de

FOTONACHWEISE / PHOTO CREDITS
Johannes Döring: S. / p. 27
Ivo Faber: S. / pp. 4–5, 59–61, 64–69, 72–73
Tobias Hoffknecht: S. / pp. 41–45
Katja Illner: S. / p. 6
Guido Kaspar: S. / pp. 20, 21, 30
Achim Kukulies: S. / pp. 71, 74–75, 84–85
Christian Teiss: S. / p. 22, und / and Maren Maurer

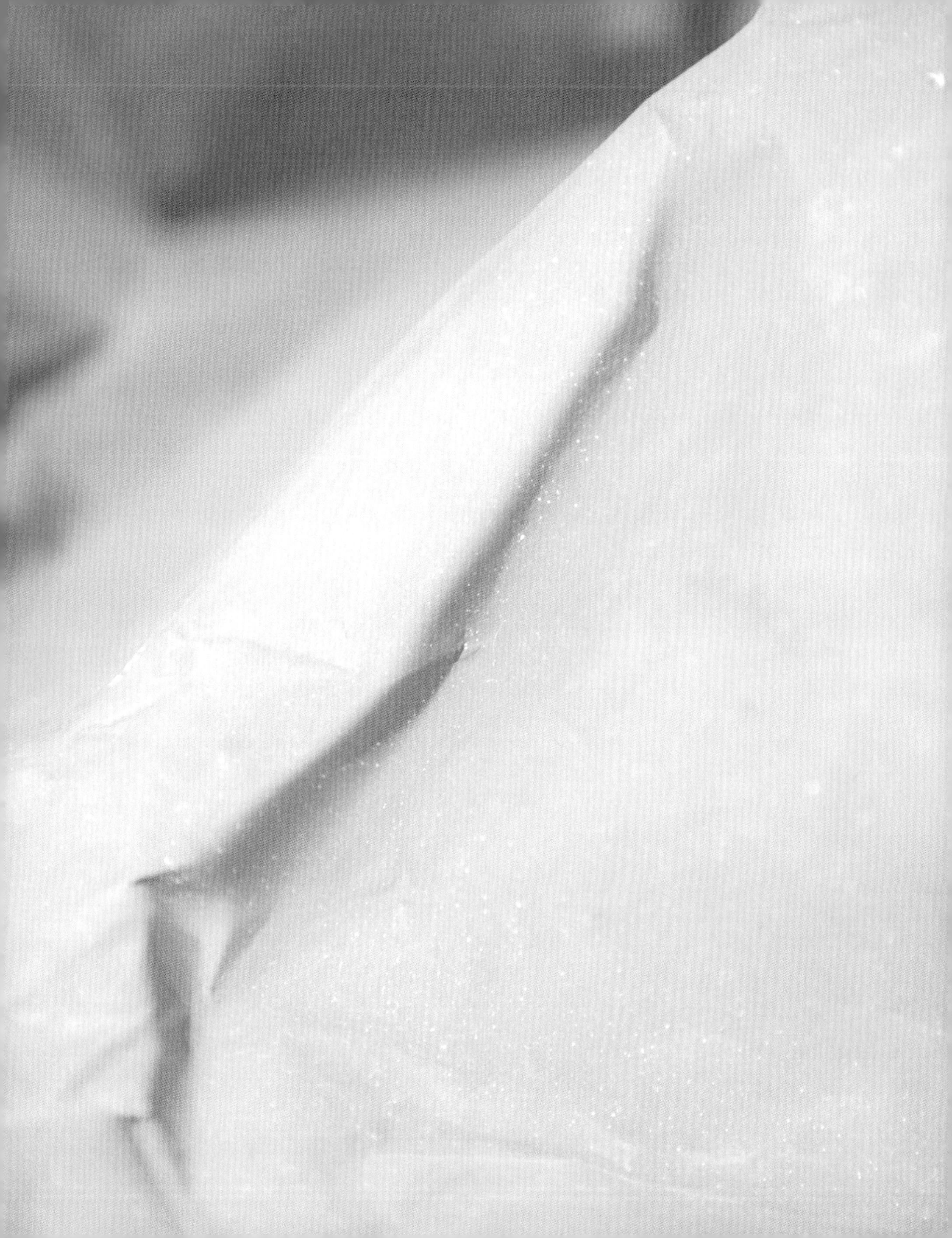

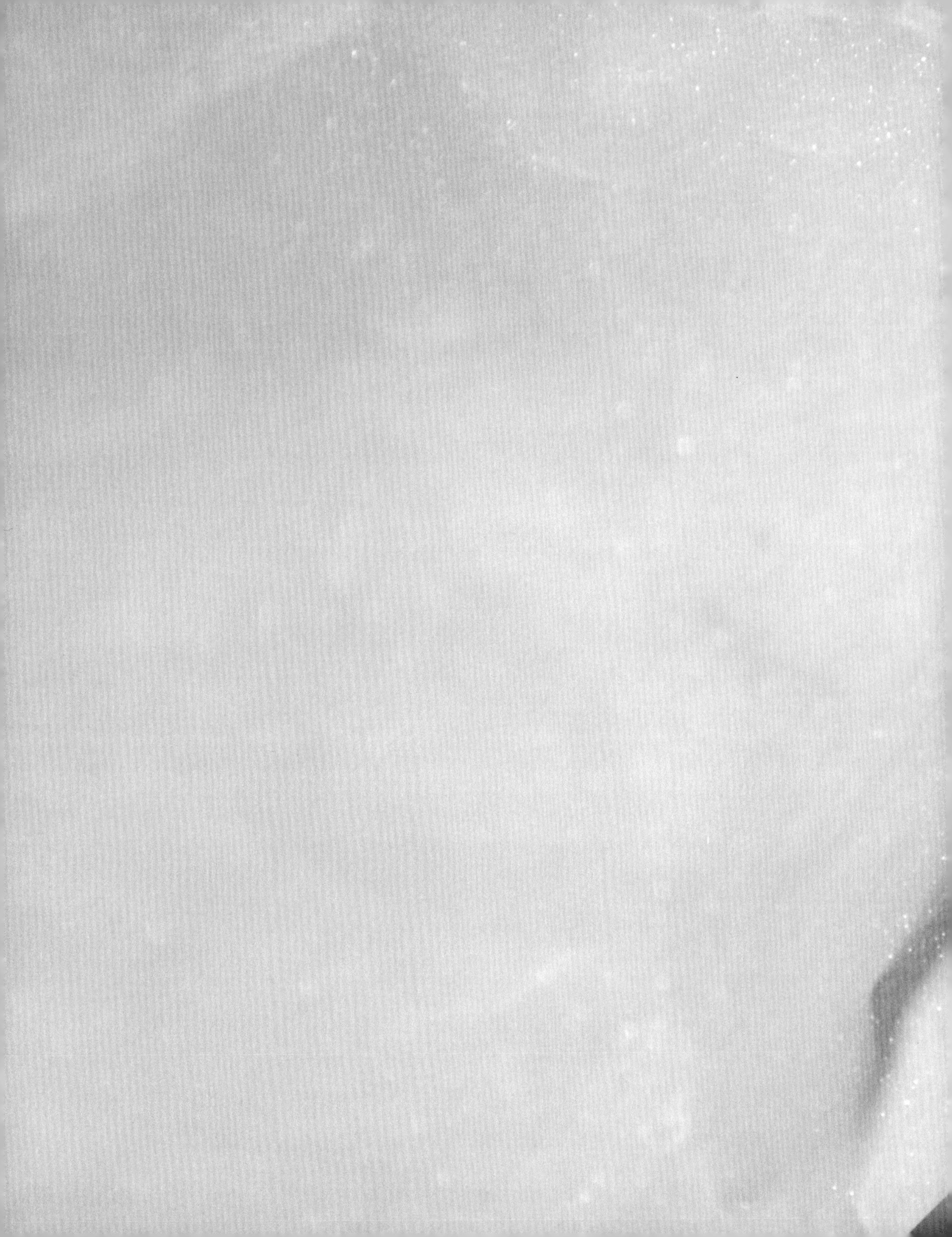